INNOVATION ABYSS

An Innovator's Solutions to Corporate Innovation Failure

Dr. Chris DeArmitt FRSC

Praise for Innovation Abyss

"This book is an essential reference for anyone interested in how Innovation really happens.

It explains the balanced role of free- and out-of-the-box thinkers, creative mavericks and visionary leaders who lead their people instead of managing them.

You will find loads of great examples, thought provoking ideas and the book is full of helpful insights."

Rob Kirschbaum – CEO SakuragiConsult
& former VP of Innovation at DSM

"Dr. DeArmitt has written an engaging, thoughtful, and provocative book about innovation.

He has drawn on his extensive personal experience at companies both large and small, recent research, and many other innovators' experiences.

The result is a framework of how companies actually operate in practice today, how that often hampers instead of helps innovation, and a set of suggestions and practical recommendations useable by individuals up to company directors."

Micah Yairi, Co-Founder & CTO, Tactus Technology

"Chris DeArmitt enjoyably relates his adventures as a true innovator in a substantially automated world.

He identifies all those structures and procedures we have installed that prevent progress from happening: it is a call for all of us working in any position in a larger organization to get our targets straight.

*Reading this book will make you laugh and cry.
It invites you to start thinking and may even make you act...if you dare...like Chris."*

Professor Gerrit Luinstra, University of Hamburg

"Really packed with useful information - with sufficient references to sources, personal and honest - plus useful advice and conclusions.

It should be on the Christmas book list of anyone serious about getting results from innovation."

Martin Whitcroft, Solutions Architect, Motorola Solutions

Printed in the United States of America

First Printing, 2016

ISBN 978-0-9978499-0-5

Phantom Plastics LLC
2 Denison Lane
Terrace Park, OH 45174
USA

Disclaimer
This publication contains the ideas and opinions of its author. It is
intended to provide helpful and informative material on the topics
addressed in the publication. It is based on the author's recollection
of events, related to the best of his knowledge. Incidents are related
to highlight problems faced by companies in general and are not
intended to portray any given company or individual in a negative
light. The author does not assume and hereby disclaims any liability
to any party for any loss, damage, or disruption caused by errors or
omissions, whether such errors or omissions result from accident,
negligence, or any other cause. If you do not agree to be bound by
this disclaimer, please discontinue reading and request a refund.

To my lovely wife Anna

&

my wonderful daughters

Ella and Leah

FOREWORD BY PROFESSOR ROGER ROTHON

Why do you need this book? According to my dictionary, Innovation is simply changing things. If that was all, then it would be really easy, we could all do it and there would be no need for help. Unfortunately, in the real world it means changing things in a useful and constructive way, which is much more challenging and meets many obstacles. We all need help to do this sort of Innovation.

Chris is a perfect person to write about Innovation in this real context, and I believe he has done it excellently in this book. Not only is it full of invaluable advice, but it is well illustrated with real examples.

Chris is one of the most creative and enthusiastic people that I have met in my own career, spanning nearly fifty years of technical problem solving and new product development. He is also very honest and loyal where it is justified, which has sometimes got him into scrapes with "management".

I have frequently used Chris's input to my own projects and he never fails to contribute. Like me, he takes joy in results that don't conform to expectations. These should never be regarded as a nuisance and are frequently the lifeblood for new approaches.

For this book, Chris has been able to draw on a wealth of experience developed in his own path from Government Institute through both large corporates and smaller companies in several countries and two continents. I have had the pleasure to correspond and sometimes work with him all this time, and have seen how he has met and overcome many of the frustrations that innovators can experience. I have also noted how, as time has progressed, he has added critical business acumen to his innate creativity.

Let him inspire you.

Professor Roger Rothon
Rothon Consultants, UK

PREFACE

Why this book? How it is different and why should you read it?

Despite the great attention paid to the topic, there has been no improvement in innovation effectiveness for decades. There are certainly more than ample books on it, so you may wonder what prompted me to write yet another one. I felt compelled to write this book to set the record straight and to give a genuine insight into how innovation works or, perhaps I should say, doesn't work. Having read many books on innovation, it is clear that they are not written by people with hands-on experience. Firstly, there are books written by innovation "experts" from the large companies. However, those companies are, frankly, pathetic at innovation. Then there are authors who are business school professors who espouse reasonable sounding theories that, unfortunately, do not describe or solve the real problems holding us back. There has been no progress for decades because we have been listening to the wrong advice.

"Experience without theory is blind, but theory without experience is mere intellectual play."
Immanuel Kant

This book is written by someone who is a proven serial innovator with deep inside experience of the fruitless innovation attempts made by companies of all sizes. The executives, I am sure, wonder how it is that no matter how much money they throw at innovation efforts, nothing seems to emerge from the much touted "innovation pipeline". This book will tell you what is going on, what is going wrong and what you can do to get dramatically better results, for far less money. By dramatic, I mean more than tenfold improvement in your ability to convert ideas into profit generating new products.

Whether you are a board member, an executive, a project manager or an innovator, you will get the real story and specific advice on what you can do to get far better results.

I started out with my shiny new PhD with a belief that the world was hungry for innovation and that increased funding would go a long way to improve the lot of countries and companies looking for a technical edge. Now, over 25 years later, I have a very different viewpoint, but how could I be sure if it was the right one? I was not initially so sure that my experiences and views could be applied across a wider range of companies and industries. Then in 2009 my friend Dr. Duane Priddy, Global Vice President at SpecialChem, invited me to present at a workshop he was holding for their members as a private event at the NPE/Antec in Chicago. SpecialChem has several hundred thousand members spanning different industries and although I was flattered, it was with some trepidation that I accepted. I had given countless talks in my areas of technical expertise but I was not sure what other industry professionals would think of my views on innovation. Sometimes you have to push beyond your comfort zone and I did that by accepting the invitation. I'm a person who always keeps a commitment, so, by accepting, I knew I would have to prepare something and then hope it was well received.

SpecialChem had booked a fairly large room for their members to come hear about innovation. I looked out over perhaps 10 or 15 round tables with a good sized group at each. I had seen talks on innovation before and they always seemed to focus on entertainment, clichés and a feel-good vibe. Anyone who knows me knows that's not my style. I tell is like it is. Brutally direct you might say. Of course, that makes it all the more nerve-racking for me. So, I launched into my talk entitled "Innovation in Industry: All Talk and No Action" starting with what innovation is and why we need it. Then I started to explain why stage-gate doesn't work, to give examples of how one bad apple employee can cost you hundreds of thousands of dollars and how today's obsession with safety is causing hugely negative and unintended consequences. By the end, the audience were not just chuckling but roaring with laughter. They laughed not because I was attempting to be amusing but because my stories resonated with them and their own struggles. Needless to say I was hugely relieved. Looking around the room, I could feel a connection to those professionals at large global companies who clearly related to my stories.

All the time I had wondered whether my personal experiences had been just bad luck. To the contrary, it became clear that the same problems apply all over the world and across different industries. After that talk and follow-up articles, I decided to keep investigating, so that I could build up a better understanding and perhaps one day publish something more substantial about innovation. What you are reading now is the culmination of that effort.

ACKNOWLEDGEMENTS

First I would like to thank my wife who prompted me to start writing after years taking notes in preparation. This journey would not have begun without that nudge.

Duane Priddy invited me to step out of my comfort zone and share my insider experience of innovation. I am grateful to Duane for his support and to SpecialChem.

Roger Rothon, a close friend and fellow innovator, has been his usual generous self by reading the manuscript drafts, making helpful suggestions and correcting errors. Thanks Roger. You're an inspiration.

Professor Norman Billingham persuaded me to study polymer science. He then inspired me with his enthusiasm and insight. He made even the most complex topics seem simple, as only a true master can.

I must also thank Dr. David Bott and Courtaulds who sponsored me through my degree and PhD. They gave me my first chance to taste corporate innovation and I loved it. Thanks.

Scott Stephenson (then at Intertech) gave me my first chance to speak at a major event and then later my first opportunity to start chairing conferences. Thank you Scott.

As for the many who shared their stories of corporate behavior, I had better refrain from naming you but you know who you are and I thank you. Only by exposing what's really going on can we hope to create a better world.

Table of Contents

INTRODUCTION

I have bad news and good news. The bad news is that your company is probably average, that is to say terrible, at innovation. The first piece of good news is that your competitors are just as ineffective. The second, even better, piece of good news is that there are fast, simple actions you can take to get a huge boost and make your company outcompete in the marketplace. It's a bold claim but as you will see, I have the proof to back it up.

I'd better spend a couple of pages explaining how I developed these opinions and why I'm confident they can help you. I have worked in companies of all sizes, including roles in R&D, Sales and Marketing, spread across several countries (England, Sweden, Italy, Germany, USA), so I have broad experience in every sense. Most importantly, I have direct experience as a serial innovator who has witnessed the rather pathetic attempts of companies to bring ideas to market.

I have read the usual books on the topic, hoping to find answers. Likely, some of the very same books you have read. Indeed, the books seem sensible enough at first glance and fun to read too. Unfortunately, they fail to accurately describe the plight of innovation efforts today and therefore, they fail to propose the right solutions.

Why are these books inadequate? The authors are sincere and well-intentioned but they tend to fall into two categories.

Firstly, there is the group consisting of people at Fortune 100 companies with the word "innovation" somewhere in their title. Ask them what they have invented, or personally brought to market and be prepared to be greeted with an awkward silence. They have no valid experience to offer. Then there are the business school professors who look at the topic from the outside, espouse theories and talk a good game. However, their advice doesn't apply out in the field because they have never been in the field. Think about it, a professor is someone who decided on a life in academia rather than the harsh challenges presented by the real world you and I live in. If you want something more than amusing anecdotes and useless theory, then read on to find out what's really holding innovation back and what you can do to unleash it.

I will share real stories from a dozen well known companies including places where I worked. Some of the stories may be amusing but the message is serious and by the end of the book you will have a clear view of the problems, renewed hope for the future, and a roadmap to success.

Every company needs innovation. It's the process of turning ideas into new products and sales to stay competitive and keep profits up. Investors look to make sure companies have a healthy innovation track record and pipeline for the future. It's a big part of the company valuation. Without it, the valuation suffers. In the long term, the company will fail to stay relevant and may eventually perish. The market is not static and our ability to innovate can be visualized as a race for progress. Races are won by being fast and having the endurance to finish. It's the same for innovation. Anything that slows us down or makes us want to give up is counterproductive and we will have no chance to win if such factors are allowed to take over.

The idea of the market clock was first introduced to my newly graduated self in the early 1990s when I took my first job at the Cookson Group at their corporate R&D site called CTC. A super guy called Steve Bold told me about the book Developing Products in Half the Time (Preston G. Smith and Donald G. Reinertsen). An excellent book by the way. Here's what it says.

"The market clock measures the time it takes us to respond to opportunities in the marketplace. It starts ticking when a customer opportunity appears and continues inexorably until the customer's need is filled. The market clock is unforgiving. It keeps on ticking whether we are working on the project or not, and with each passing minute we pay the cost of delay."

That is a powerful image and it has stayed with me throughout my career. When I have a really good idea, that has major value, I hear that clock ticking. There is value there and it's only a matter of time before my competitor sees it and beats me to the punch. Big companies seem to think that the world is waiting for them to finish their extended coffee break or endless meetings. The market is not waiting for them and that's why the small, hungry companies often win the race.

What do I see within companies? I see people working on the wrong projects, taking far too long about it and finally, with luck, delivering something to pass on to Product Development or Production people who have no interest in it because it wasn't invented by them. If by some miracle, and it is a minor miracle to get that far, the product makes it into production, Marketing have lost interest or the market needs have moved on. The window of opportunity is no longer open. If you're an executive, you may think I'm being overly negative, but let me assure you, this is exactly how it's being run now in your organization. If you work on innovation projects, then you already know it's true.

So, if this really is a race, then what does it take to win a race? Easy! You need to be pointed in the right direction and then you need to run quickly. Cue mental flashback to the Monty Python race for people with no sense of direction. Joking aside, we will now look at how to be sure we are fast and focused. This book reveals the roadblocks, so that they may be removed or ameliorated. It will transform your innovation efforts from mundane to marvelous.

IDEAS

Introduction

I deas are the launching point for the innovation process. Every company needs a plentiful source of ideas. Once they have been collected, it is then crucial to select the best ones and be able to tweak them to fit the market needs and the company strategy. This section will look at all of these aspects. Firstly, we will look at how and where to get great ideas at the lowest cost. We will challenge the notion that one needs a large internal R&D unit. It turns out that huge savings are possible. Then we will examine the vital role of idea selection and tuning. As we will see, this latter aspect alone can multiply your success rate almost tenfold.

The opening cartoon alludes to an essential topic - speed. Given enough time, a competitor will eventually have the idea too. The art of successful innovation isn't just having the ideas but getting them to market before someone else patents it to block you, or gains a lead by commercializing faster. If your company is quicker at creating new products than your rivals, then you will out-compete them. That is exactly the focus of this book. After reading it, you will have all the information needed to generate a huge and sustainable lead over your rivals.

IDEA CREATION

"The best way to have a good idea is to have a lot of ideas."
Linus Pauling

It is essential to generate a lot of ideas because it has been shown that 3000 raw ideas are needed to eventually generate one money-making new product (Stevens and Burley 1997). Those are shocking numbers and later we will look at proven methods to get wildly better results than that. Idea creation is not so easy though.

We start off in life very creative but then we spend years in school where we are trained to conform. Think of how many times children are told not to do something. Every one of those admonitions is a request for conformity. I have children, so I am acutely aware of the need for some rules and guidance. However, it turns out that the way children are brought up beats the creativity out of them (A. Grant 2016). It has been proven, for example, that teachers disfavor the creative children. If you ask the teachers directly, they claim to like creative kids, perhaps because that's the politically correct answer. However, when you actually ask them to say which specific traits they value, it turns out that creativity is not appreciated (A. Grant in Originals). Why is that? I can speculate that it's a lot less work for a teacher to have a room full of quiet, passive kids than to deal with the unpredictability and extra work engendered by creative children. I highly suspect that it's the same for adults in the workplace where managers in corporations prefer the easy life.

For a very nice presentation of this phenomenon I highly recommend the book Orbiting the Giant Hairball, written by a creative artist who worked at Hallmark Cards for 30 years. He gives a moving description of how it is to be a creative person in the grip of a corporate giant. Giant Hairball that is. He also shares his experience of asking school children whether they are an artist. In their first year of school, almost all kids think of themselves as an artist, that is to say creative, but after just a few years of school, hardly any will admit to it. Extrapolate that and imagine the trace of creativity remaining when, several years later, such people are finally ready to join the workforce. Most have already been beaten into passivity.

It is commonly believed that discoveries happen via chance and that scientists should be given free scope to pursue whatever direction they choose. I was born in the US and grew up in the UK. My stepfather, Sir Howard Dalton FRS, was a university professor and so I was brought up with the impression that science was underfunded and that it was the responsibility of the government to increase funding to protect the future of the country. That sounded very sensible to me as a youngster.

The attitude in the UK, where I studied for my degree and PhD, is that pure science is best and that applied science is somehow dirty and of lesser worth. That is a great shame and an even greater mistake. It encourages pure science, meaning science with no real purpose, over science that can actually help people, companies, and society. There is a public perception that we must fund pure scientists to do "blue sky" work and that they will stumble upon something great. We should work to change that misguided perception so that the applied scientists are respected and appreciated.

So, what is my opinion now that I've seen science in action for some decades? Throughout my career, I've seen far too many adult scientists playing around. Some companies have giant R&D teams just burning through cash with no real hope or intention of delivering meaningful innovation. It's more like a mini university than a meaningful industrial research effort. This should be identified and stopped because it does not give value to the shareholders.

> *"Basic research is like shooting an arrow in the air and, where it lands, painting a target."*
> Homer Adkins (Nature, 1984)

In my view, applied science is of much more value and it is unquestionably very much harder. Burning through cash without purpose is easy. Applied research is not, for many reasons. For one, you don't get to choose the problem you work on. Furthermore, you have to solve it on a schedule, with limited resources and the solution has to be safe, inexpensive and possible to implement in production without major investment. Now that is a challenge.

Where do the ideas come from? You might assume that the majority of ideas come from R&D but in fact, that is not the case (IBM Study 2006). A study showed that R&D did not contribute nearly as much as other sources such as customers. People also argue about market push versus market pull, with advocates for each. In my view, neither is optimal. Market push means creating something you want to produce because it fits with your capabilities and then hoping the customer wants it. Market pull too often means asking the customer what they want, i.e. "voice of the customer". The problem there is that the customer doesn't know what is possible. I bet plenty of customers would ask for a car that does 500 miles per gallon but that's not technically feasible. As we shall see later, neither market push nor pull can work alone. Only the combination of the two can yield results.

You might also ask which function in the company should be generating ideas. Here are my observations.

- R&D know what's technically possible but don't know what the market needs
- Marketing people claim to know what the customer wants but ironically, in many companies, the Marketing people have never even met a customer
- Sales people may know what the market wants because they meet customers regularly but they don't know what's technically possible
- The managers usually know neither what's possible nor what's wanted

This is clearly a challenge. So who is able to generate feasible ideas that address real needs? Only someone who has experience of both the technical side and the market needs can be consistently effective. The optimal person is a so-called polymath or "Renaissance man" (or woman of course). Leonardo da Vinci, Sir Isaac Newton, and Galileo are famous examples. Those people with deep interest and expertise in more than one area are rare. Furthermore, they do not fit into the boxes ordained by big company structures. In a corporation you are in R&D, or Marketing, or Sales, or Management. Thus, the very structure of the company prevents progress. In smaller companies that is not the case. In smaller companies, there are not enough staff to warrant a rigid organizational structure and instead the attitude is usually, "just get it done". No-one cares who does it, as long as it happens and that goes for every activity all the way down to emptying the trash.

In a larger company, the rules of probability dictate that you have average employees and therefore an average amount of ideas per employee. If you choose to, you can be different and actually do something with those ideas. By that I mean have a system to collect them, reward people for them, screen them and be seen to act on them. Even that small effort would give you an advantage over standard companies, i.e. your competitors. You could also try to generate more ideas by hiring more people but that is a very expensive approach. In the section on Open Innovation we prove that it is far, far cheaper and more effective to look externally for additional ideas.

Instead of hiring a statistically average set of full-time employees, you could instead try to get an above average talent base. In my experience, large companies, like BASF, tend to believe that they are above average. In fact, they are not. Big companies build castles where their people are sheltered. They believe they are superior because, for example, they are the best in their department, but are not exposed to truly world-class competition. It's like being the village skiing champion. That's great but it doesn't qualify you to enter, let alone win, the Olympics. Your company needs world-class ideas to compete on a global stage.

Once you have assembled a collection of ideas, then the key to success is being able to tell the good ones from the not so good ones. I remember when I was a teenager, I was already having lots of ideas, but it's hard to have world-class ideas when you are so young because you don't yet know enough. You don't have a big enough toolkit at your disposal to craft the best ideas.

Also, you don't yet know what is already out there, nor the unaddressed needs. Over the years, my raw creativity may have actually declined but my production of valuable output has increased dramatically. That's due, in large part, to an improved ability to judge what ideas are most likely to work, which ones take least effort to realize and which of those address known market needs. Improvement there has helped tremendously. It wasn't easy and it took years to get there. I have to give credit to my stepfather. When I was a teenager, he said that there is a gap between the scientists who create what no-one needs and their managers who can't make good decisions about what to prioritize because they don't understand the science. He told me that if I could bridge that gap, it would be of enormous value. It was a powerful message and that became my goal.

I started off with creativity and spent years practicing to become better at the business side. It is my fervent belief that such dual-functional people, I call them "Effectuators" (in honor of Jack Vance, a favorite author), have the potential to bring an enormous edge to an organization. They do so by spanning the gaps between the corporate functions. The Stars of the Big Screen section talks more about the value of such dual-functional people.

> *"Eagles don't fit in pigeon holes."*
> Chris DeArmitt

Do you know the problem with being an Effectuator? There is no such position in most organizations. When I look for a job, I can either choose the expert role and use that part of my skill set, or I can choose a management role and use those skills. Both roles have a notional salary cap, so there is no way to get paid extra for bringing the combination of skills. Again, by putting everything in neat boxes, large organizations block even

13

the possibility of having a difference maker. Small companies are less strict. Staff are often allowed to do whatever needs to be done, regardless of official title. That gives them an edge and provides a more enjoyable environment for creative types to work in.

Another effect may be at play here too. Smaller companies are often under resourced, so getting tasks done is a mad scramble. It could be that the lack of time in a small company forces everything to be done last minute, thereby improving the end result because pressure improves performance. It should be noted that while working under some pressure has been proven to be advantageous, that is only true up to a point. Extreme pressure is not positive.

Companies should strive to hire creative types and make sure to reward the high performing individuals. Also, as we shall see, many companies are set up in such a way as to drive out the best performers. That will be described later in more detail.

G. Stevens and J. Burley, "3000 Raw Ideas = 1 Commercial Success!" Research•Technology Management, 40(3): 16-27, May-June, 1997.

How to Raise a Creative Child. Step One: Back Off, Adam Grant, New York Times, January 30th 2016.

Originals: How Non-Conformists Move the World, Adam M. Grant, Viking (Random House), New York USA, 2016.

IBM The Global CEO Study 2006 based on interviews with 765 CEOs and business leaders.

Seek the Seventh Sigma

"Consistency is the last refuge of the unimaginative."
Oscar Wilde

Six Sigma is hugely popular. It's a term borrowed from mathematics and refers to the application of strict procedures and processes to ensure predictable outcomes i.e. a very low defect rate. I view it as making sure everything is normal and within a defined box and I have to agree, that concept does seem to have merit for repetitive processes like mass production.

As we know, innovation is the exact opposite of a predictable, repeatable process and we often hear the phrase "outside the box". I like to think of innovation as "the seventh sigma", the extraordinary outcomes, existing outside the norm. Seeking that seventh sigma is the correct course of action when we want a breakthrough.

Evolution works the same way. Normally, DNA works perfectly and we get exact copies as planned but every now and then, a chance variation leads to a breakthrough. If DNA were to become perfect and stop making errors, evolution would stop. Think about that for a moment. Tolerance of change, i.e. innovation is essential for our existence and future survival.

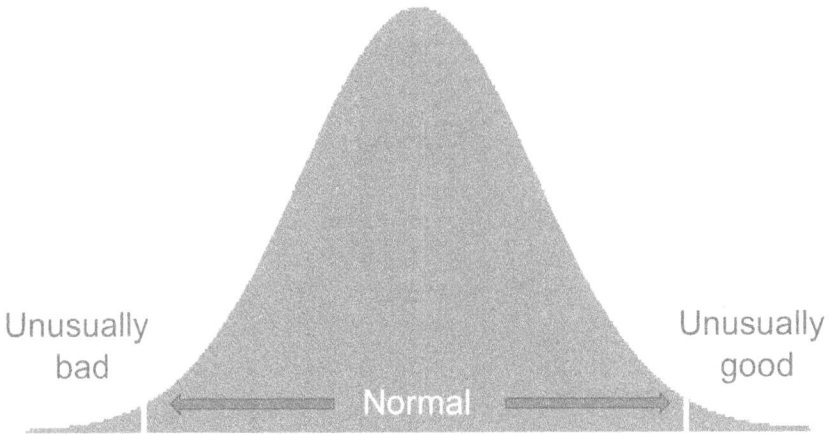

Distribution - 6 sigma is the normal, 7th sigma is extraordinary

While writing this, I saw an article talking about how 3M implemented Six Sigma some years ago, not only in production but in R&D as well (Dodge 2007). They were surprised to find that all innovation stopped and they eventually had to reverse the decision. The article is handy for me because I can cite it in support of my case. It was concluded that Six Sigma is effective at what it is intended to do, but that it is "narrowly designed to fix an existing process" and does not help in "coming up with new products or disruptive technologies." (Richardson 2007).

This should have been obvious to anyone with modest intelligence but apparently the leaders of one of the world's largest corporations didn't find it so. I'm not sure what conclusions to draw from that. Apparently, it didn't occur to them that a process for tight control doesn't work for a creative activity. Furthermore, it didn't occur to them to ask for evidence that Six Sigma actually works before implementing it. As we have seen, the evidence proves that it is severely detrimental. What companies sometimes see is an initial improvement when implementing Six Sigma and then a decline because it killed new product creation. Perhaps, in todays short term world, executives are happy to implement a process that gives a quick gain and receive a handsome bonus in return? Let's look at the efficacy of Six Sigma.

A Fortune article stated that "of 58 large companies that have announced Six Sigma programs, 91 percent have trailed the S&P 500 since". I checked into that and the study behind it was never published, so I did some more digging and found this topic has been investigated thoroughly. One hundred and eight Fortune 500 were analyzed by Ozkan, Davis and Hassan in a 2014 report. Some of their findings are quoted below.

"This finding indicates that the billions claimed as cost savings by Six Sigma companies do not carry down to the bottom line."

"Findings show that Six Sigma companies indeed outperformed the market and exceeded the S&P index. However, Six Sigma company performance was not on parity with firms of similar size in the same industries."

That reminds me of this apt comment...

"However beautiful the strategy, you should occasionally look at the results."
Winston Churchill

Apparently, Six Sigma does not provide an edge and the leaders forgot to check whether it works.

Coming back to the seventh sigma. We know that seventh sigma events are statistically improbable, so how will we intentionally create them? We could wait a long time and hope for a random event, i.e. a miracle. However, that would give us no competitive advantage and good business plans should not depend on miracles. Try explaining that "hope for a miracle" strategy to the shareholders.

Where do we look to find creativity? I interviewed quite a few people for this book and asked them for their heartfelt thoughts on innovation. One of my friends, who is an MBA and has worked in major companies gave his views. His first comment? He said, "they seem to think that they can put the word innovation in someone's title and expect them to deliver." He said he's never seen anyone with such a title deliver anything. Neither have I. Creativity is either in your blood, or it isn't.

There are plenty of books, courses and tools to help you become more creative. Such exercises can be fun and they do generate ideas. However, it has been proven that creative inclination is genetic, so training is not the right approach. A training session will not create a world-class ideas person. In my view, that should be obvious. If I want to create a hit song should I go to Björn and Benny, the proven hit generators from ABBA and multiple musicals, or should I give someone off the street a tambourine and have them beat on it for 20 minutes in a meeting room? I think we all know which is more likely to generate positive results.

The way to get access to world-class ideas people is to hire more of them either full-time, or as consultants. Then cast a wider net and access others around the world, as we shall see in the Open Innovation chapter, coming up next.

———————————————

Dodge, John (10 December 2007). "3M Shelves Six Sigma in R&D". Design News. Retrieved 2013-04-02.

Betsy Morris, New rule: Look out, not in. Old rule: Be lean and mean. FORTUNE Magazine 2006.

Six Sigma, Stock Returns and Operating Performance, Bora Ozkan, J. Ronnie Davis, and Kabir M. Hassan, Temple University 2014.

Richardson, Karen (7 January 2007). "The 'Six Sigma' Factor for Home Depot". Wall Street Journal Online. Retrieved 2007-10-15.

Open Innovation

"The opportunities of man are limited only by his imagination. But so few have imagination that there are ten thousand fiddlers to one composer."

Charles F. Kettering

Open Innovation is all the rage. It is simply a way to buy ideas from outside your company. Although the concept is widely known and the practice relatively widespread, here, for the first time, you will see actual numbers to quantify its value.

Companies like BASF employ thousands of R&D people. Each has a degree and many have a PhD. That means enormous expense and only a very few of those people give any valuable breakthroughs. As an example, of all those I knew at BASF, only one, a good friend Graham McKee retired with over 200 patents including some with major commercial importance. I was lucky to spend time with him creating new products and processes. Xerox has one such inventor called Santokh Badesha who received an award for reaching over 100 patents. Even the world's largest companies have just one or two prolific inventors. These are the few and your chances of employing even one are not good at all. How much would it cost to try and get just one? I can tell you the answer.

Open Innovation brokers like Innocentive® post problems and needs from large companies and collect potential solutions from their members from around the world. If the company sees a solution they like, then they pay out a cash prize and the inventor transfers patent rights to the solution seeker. It's a simple concept, but does it really pay off? Should your company be doing it too? As it happens, I can answer that too, based on my own experiences as an Open Innovation problem solver.

To date, I have solved 6 open innovation challenges with Innocentive®. Only 40 people out of their 275 000 registered innovators have achieved that amount of success. That means one out of 6800, i.e. 0.01%. The implication is that you would need to hire, on average, 6800 innovation employees to get just one with that level of value-adding creativity. If we assume a conservative salary of just $50,000 per employee, to employ 6000 people would cost well over 300 million dollars per year. That doesn't even guarantee you will get that one special individual, you might get two, or none at all. Think about that, 300 million per year in salaries just for a chance to make a breakthrough. No wonder large corporations are frustrated at their inability to get a return on their R&D spending!

The CTO of a huge company once told me that he didn't believe in open innovation. I found that surprising. It's like saying you'd rather pay that 300 million per year in fixed salary costs instead of paying a few tens of thousands per year in open innovation challenge awards. Crazy. The advantages don't stop there. With open innovation, you get access to hundreds of thousands of potential solvers and you only pay if you get a solution you are satisfied with! Those solvers come from all kinds of backgrounds and that diversity offers the ability to see problems from a new angle. Often the corporate R&D people are blinkered by years at the same job and are unable to offer a fresh perspective. You're paying the salaries for 5999 who are not generating results, just to get that one person who gives you an occasional breakthrough. Ironically, that one person who delivers is usually not rewarded for it, but more on that later.

Would you rather spend over 300 million in fixed costs every year for the hope of one difference maker or pay one thousandth of that in prize money to an external person and only if they presented you with a great solution? Apparently, that CTO would prefer the first option.

That's the beauty of open innovation. After all, where do you think the people with the "out of the box" ideas are? They are usually to be found outside of the box! By that I mean that they are outside your organization and you need to search externally to find them. You and they will be happier keeping it that way because it's cheaper for you and the truly creative people often prefer to be outside the confines of corporations.

Open innovation can be extremely effective but it is not a panacea. For example, of the many open innovation companies I have worked with as a solver, only one of them, Innocentive®, has actually paid off. As a leading solver for Innocentive® I know my solutions are world-class, so what went wrong when I worked with those other companies? There are two main problems I've encountered.

Firstly, the reward system has to be set up correctly. Some open innovation companies pay the solver nothing until the product is made and generates sales. That, as we shall see later, is an extreme long shot, due to corporate inability to successfully commercialize products. The premise is that the solver gets a royalty on sales. However, that is likely to be never, or at best, many years down the road. By which time I suspect everyone has forgotten where the idea came from. I have solved problems for companies that used that model and I have not received anything so far. Years from now if they do commercialize, it would be very hard for me to prove that I am owed money. I have therefore given up on open innovation companies using that model.

Secondly, there is a problem when it comes to recognizing the best solution. You may present something very good to the client. You may even know for a fact that it works but as we will see in this book, companies are truly awful at recognizing good ideas that can lead to profitable products. One must remember that the people judging your ideas are, I hate to say it, the same people who were too stupid, lazy or lacking in imagination, to come up with the solution themselves. That can be a major hurdle.

I should probably give you an example to show just how real this issue can be. I was hired as a consultant to a very large plastic manufacturer. They make the plastic granules which are then melted and molded by others to make the products you and I buy in the shop. Anyway, I flew in to their site and presented for a team of about ten people. They had asked me how to make better plastics and they had one particular request. They wanted ideas on how to make their plastic more impact resistant so it wouldn't break when dropped, for example. Of course, they wanted the solution to be cheap and the additive had to be effective in very low doses. Not an easy challenge considering that giant companies like DuPont had been trying to do the very same thing for decades with giant R&D teams behind their efforts. I was expected to come up with this revolutionary technology in two weeks, with no budget for experiments.

I did present an idea during the meeting and said it had a reasonable chance of working, citing some evidence from

23

books. Not only was the reaction unenthusiastic, one person actually became quite rude. She stated that my contribution and visit was a waste of time. I remained unflustered and smiled enigmatically, or at least that's how I hope it looked. I went home and heard nothing for many months.

Then the friend who had invited me called and said he had been reading the patents from their arch rivals. Their nemesis had just patented the exact technology I had proposed and showed that it worked beautifully, just as I had suggested. He showed his colleagues what a mistake they had made by not listening. They were unable to recognize the solution handed to them on a plate with proof that it should work.

The story ended there, or so I thought. Two years later I was chatting to their arch rival and asked if they had any pressing needs. The guy said, "yes, we need to find an additive that can be used in very low amounts, to improve the impact resistance of our plastic". I said, you already have it. Your colleague patented it two years ago! He had not heard about it, so I had to tell him to go see his colleague who worked 5 offices down the hallway. What a story huh? You couldn't make it up if you tried.

From this we see that companies may not be able to recognize a good idea, even one that they have paid an expert for, i.e. open innovation. We have also seen just how bad communication and corporate memory are.

A colleague at BASF once opened his filing cabinet and showed me all the reports he had written over the years. He said "I could republish one every week for the rest of my career and everyone would think it was new work". I believe him.

Open innovation is not limited to new ideas. It extends to new technologies as well. Often when new ideas are purchased, they fail because they are left to navigate the corporate innovation maze outlined in this book. Instead, it is possible to access validated solutions where a great deal of the work has already been done. I think of it as analogous to buying a tree. I can buy a seed for very low cost but will it germinate? If it does, then the seedling will be vulnerable and if it does survive, I will have a long wait before I can enjoy the shade of a fully grown tree. One must strike a balance between budget and time. I recently did some work in my garden and purchased small trees instead of seeds. I paid up to get faster results with less risk.

Technologies work the same way. In many cases, it makes more sense to go buy a solution that's ready to go. It sounds sensible but where does one shop for new technologies? You can't go to the supermarket to get them. The vast majority of new technologies come from lone inventors and smaller companies. Those people have solutions to sell but usually, they have no path to get them to market. I know that frustration from my early career, before my network was fully developed. You have the solution, you know the market needs it and yet you can't get it in front of the prospective customer.

Earlier in the book we talked about Effectuators, my word for people who cross boundaries. They are facilitators who accelerate progress by making connections. That's just what we need here and that need is filled by, for example, Leading Edge Only (LEO). They provide a service that matches solutions to prospective clients. Not only is it a great resource but they have spent a lot of effort making the system look appealing and fun to use. You can quickly grasp the technologies on offer and take it from there.

Of course, it is possible to get your new technology to market on your own without help but from my experience, that is a painful path. Every truly new materials breakthrough I have seen, took about 15 years to find its killer application and gain meaningful commercial traction. If you have a lot of patience and deep pockets, that's fine but even as I write this, I know of one small company that is at the end of 15 years and running out of funding. They may not make it to the end of this year. I think that the LEO approach will not only help companies flourish by accelerating commercialization but make the process more rewarding for everyone.

STARS OF THE BIG SCREEN

"True genius resides in the capacity for evaluation of uncertain, hazardous, and conflicting information."

Winston Churchill

This section reveals a proven method for improving your ability to convert ideas into profitable products by a factor of ten! When I set out to write this book I knew from my own experience that filtering ideas was a skill that dramatically improves results. However, I had no independent proof, nor a proven method to generate experts at idea screening, i.e. "stars of the big screen".

First let's look at the numbers. These findings make up the Universal Success Curve, so named because no matter which method is used, the results come out the same. This then is the dire situation companies the world over are faced with. One can see that there is tremendous room for improvement here.

Stage of New Business Development	Number of Ideas
1 – Raw, unwritten ideas	3000
2 – Submitted ideas	300
3 – Small projects	125
4 – Early stage developments	9
5 – Major developments	4
6 – Launches	1.7
7 – Successes (profitable launches)	1

This work was done at Dow® on scores of projects where they thoroughly tracked results, including profit generated. They took stage number 4 as the reference point and noted that nine stage-four projects are needed to create one successful, profitable launch, i.e. an 11% effectiveness for R&D efforts. They were able to improve that to 95% effectiveness. The improvement was so dramatic that it turns out you can cut your total R&D spending by 50% and still get better results than you have today. How did they do it? What's the secret?

They found that the key was a certain type of person with a very specific combination of skills. That special person is able to accurately predict which ideas have most merit, plus they have the ability to guide projects by morphing promising ideas into winning, profitable ideas. They found that these three qualities were essential.

- High creativity
- Deep technical expertise
- Business acumen

As you can imagine, it is almost impossible to find such a person, which they called a business opportunity analyst. As you have read, I spent my career as a highly creative and technically skilled person intentionally forcing myself to learn business skills in order to become more effective. That worked for me but how did the experts at Dow do it?

How would one set about finding people with the aptitude to be an effective technology screener and how would they be trained? Is it best to start with someone with business skills and teach creativity and technical expertise or should one do the reverse, i.e. start with the creative expert and teach them the business side, as in my own case? I had that very question while researching for this book and started looking to see whether the answer is known. I couldn't believe it when I found this very topic has been investigated and the results are not only shocking but revolutionary.

It has been shown that creativity is genetic. You don't inherit it directly but it has been found that up to 80% of creative potential is related to your genes. That means it is not effective to start with a business person and teach them to be super creative. It won't work. Therefore, we must start with someone creative and teach them the business skills. How do we identify those creative people reliably? Well, it turns out that has been discovered too.

I remember a job interview many years ago in Sweden (for ABB) where they did a quick test and identified me as "very creative and even more creative when under pressure". I was fascinated by the accuracy of a 15 minute test. I don't know what test they used all those years ago but studies have proven that popular personality tests can accurately measure creativity. In the US at least, the Myers Briggs Type Indicator® personality test is the most widely used. Many people already know their MBTI® scores. It has been found that those scores can be used to accurately estimate a person's creativity. One such method is the Creativity Index.

The Dow workers, one of whom now runs WinOvations, showed that a different calculation, dubbed the Rainmaker[SM] Index, was more accurate. In a study performed over ten years and across 267 projects, they showed that "analysts in the upper third of the Rainmaker Index generated 95 times more profit than those in the lower third." Furthermore, nearly all profits were generated by business opportunity analysts with a Myers Briggs "NT" type personality. They created $6M in profit versus only $0.7M for all the other types combined (NF, SJ, SP). When you consider that only about 12% of the population has an NT type personality, it starts to become clear why innovation struggles. There are only a few with the natural ability to navigate the "fuzzy front end" and even those few still need to be trained in business skills to be at their most effective.

The research was extremely thorough and valuable. It has all been published and I highly recommend reading it. It is amazing to me that companies seem to be oblivious to this powerful information. It is the key to unlocking far better results.

As we have seen, the work by Stevens and Swogger is proof that dramatically better innovation output is there for the taking. That being the case, why has this not been adopted across the corporate landscape? Firstly, it seems that many have not found the information. I also wonder whether people can bring themselves to believe that it is really true. You might then wonder why I accepted their findings so readily. The answer is simple. I have spent my career doing just what they describe. As a Myers Briggs ENTJ personality type, I have been astounded to see how many nonsensical projects are run. On the positive side, I have been able to generate an idea and get that through proof of concept and on to first sales in as little as a month or two. No business case, no project and sometimes without any funding. I know for sure that what Stevens and Swogger discovered is true because it mirrors what I already know from decades of experience. Let me give a few examples to illustrate the point.

When I worked at BASF, there was a department meeting when a friend and talented scientist presented his project on raising the softening temperature of a plastic so it could be used at higher temperatures. He explained that the challenge was to not raise the melting point of the plastic at the same time because the customers would not like that. What's the problem with that project? The problem is that if you take every plastic and plot a graph of softening temperature against melting point, you get a straight line. It's shown in more that one popular book, so it's not a secret. The two are very closely related and it is therefore fundamentally impossible to change one without changing the other. Thus, a large project at BASF, run by plastics experts was an utter waste of time and money. It should never have been started. That wasn't the only example I've seen when it comes to impossible projects.

Another example of misdirected R&D effort comes from Hybrid Plastics. One year, the R&D department created about 50 new molecules to add to their product catalogue. These people were very talented PhD chemists and that was quite an achievement. I created one new product. Within a month my product had significant sales and the other 50 had none. Why? Because they had made products that the market didn't need. Soon after, my product went on to be a best seller. Making new products is fun but if no-one wants them, it's a waste of effort. My best guess at that time was that my product would be good for cosmetics, so I wrote an article in a cosmetics magazine and presented the product at a cosmetics conference in California. That was a strange experience for me as a plastics expert but it's where I thought the target audience would be. Fast forward a few years and the biggest application for that product is in mascara made by one of the leading cosmetics companies.

How fast can innovation go when a single person can create ideas, judge their merit, and know the market needs? The answer is very fast indeed. Several times in my career I have gone from new product request to proof of concept and through to sales in one or two months with no project and no red tape, just results. That is fun indeed.

"If you pick the right people and give them the opportunity to spread their wings and put compensation as a carrier behind it you almost don't have to manage them."
Jack Welch

BASF Venture Capital would get all kinds of people asking them for an investment and they would pass some of the proposals to me for screening. I would tell them whether the technology made sense and whether the people involved seemed capable of pulling it off. I enjoyed that role. It amazes me that other Venture Capital companies don't engage NT types to screen for them. Their return on investment would sky-rocket. Instead, I see investments in technologies that are nonsensical.

Just last year, an investor came to me to do some due diligence. They told me that I needn't look at the technology itself because that was solid beyond question but asked whether I could anticipate anything new coming along and disrupting it. It's dangerous to make assumptions, so I checked into the technology aspect anyway. A one hour patent search showed me that their IP was worthless. They had two types of patents. Patents that were invalid due to prior art and patents that were valid but on topics of no commercial value. When I looked further into their technology I found more problems. It performed the same as other well-known, cheaper materials. Amazingly, there were already millions of dollars from a major company behind this technological lemon. The client didn't want to hear that news but he called in a patent lawyer who verified my findings. It's so quick and inexpensive to have an expert do some screening, it surprises me that companies don't spend a few dollars to protect their huge investments.

That same year, a senior executive approached me because he needed help. He and a friend of his had taken a patent on a new product for swimming pools. They had the basic idea patented and wanted some advice on the materials selection. I never accept a job before I am pretty sure I can help, so I started doing some web research. In 15 minutes I discovered that the product they were developing was for sale on Amazon from multiple vendors. They had wasted over a year of time and quite some money all because they didn't do their homework. This is the kind of futile work that can be avoided by hiring an expert, especially an "NT" type who can tell what makes sense. You can't push back the frontier unless you know where the frontier is. They had no problem spending time and money on that wild goose chase but interestingly, I was not paid a dime for saving them from further futility.

Speaking of screening, one of the US states wanted to encourage small business innovation by giving cash awards to worthy technologies. It would be used to help fund scale-up to give a working prototype. They realized that they were not qualified to choose which technologies should be funded, so they contracted outside experts and I was one of them. I was actually quite impressed at their perspicacity. So, I was given technologies to screen, sent in by universities and small companies. What did I see?

- People asking for money to develop something already on the market, i.e. available off-the-shelf
- Ideas that were clearly impossible
- Ideas that were possible but not cost competitive
- Ideas that were possible but not manufacturable
- Lastly, good ideas with both technical merit and commercial potential

Overall I'd say about one fifth had real merit. I give a lot of credit to that US State because they did find experts who were able to help make sure the public money was spent wisely. Today I saw a LinkedIn posting that the UK government had allocated £15M to "innovative R&D" projects. I couldn't help thinking that, unless they are being screened by the right people, it will be one giant waste of tax payer's money.

Bringing new products to market is fast and easy if you have the right type of people doing it and remove the barriers, such as excessive admin work. This is the way forward for any company wanting to make progress. In my experience, there is a major problem that arises. Companies don't want to reward such individuals who create enormous value for them. Almost every time I have delivered, I have been disappointed by the outright lies and pathetic arguments used to explain why I could not get fairly compensated. More on that subject later.

Based on my experiences, I wondered how they had managed to keep the NT type difference makers in the Dow study. They stated "Management made sure to reward these individuals well in their new roles, due to their scarcity, and due to the critical role they play in creating tomorrow's new business." That makes sense and I'm glad that they recognized the need to do the right thing. NT difference makers are not gullible. They have the business skills to know their own value and won't fall for the usual, rather unconvincing, arguments used to keep pay low. Dow recognized that such people are scarce (NT is about 12% of the population), they bring enormous value to the fuzzy front end and it has been shown that they evaluate twice the number of projects compared to other personality types. That last point alone means they are worth double the salary before you factor in that their results are 10x better!

The revelations about NT type people don't end there. The researchers also looked to see the fate of the difference makers when a downturn forced lay-offs. They discovered that 50% of the NT people were let go. In contrast, 100% of the other people, who do not deliver any profitable innovation, were kept. That means that companies already doing so badly that they are forced into downsizing, are dooming themselves to future failure by ejecting their potential saviors. That is very interesting information for investors to be aware of.

"Be more tolerant of the difficult people. They're the creative ones. They're not happy with the status quo."
Terry Leahy, former CEO of Tesco

Stevens, Gregory A. and James Burley. 3000 Raw Ideas = 1 Commercial Success! Research-Technology Management 40(3), 1997, pp. 16–27.

Stevens, Greg and James Burley, Piloting the Rocket of Radical Innovation, Research Technology Management 46(2), 2003, pp. 16–25.

Stevens, Greg, James Burley and Kurt Swogger, Dow Chemical Achieves Major Transformation of PO&E R&D Group: Personality-Oriented Approach Improves NPD Results. PDMA Visions XXVII, No. 3, 2003, pp. 6–10.

Stevens, Greg and Kurt Swogger, Creating a Winning R&D Culture – I, Research Technology Management, 52(1), 2009, pp. 35-50.

Stevens, G. A., and Swogger, K., Creating a Winning R&D Culture — II, Research-Technology Management, 52(3), 2009, pp. 22–28.

THE APPLE CORE

No book on innovation would be complete without some comment on the Apple phenomenon. They are the outlier because they are large and have still innovated over an extended period, wowing us with new paradigm-changing products. I have a house full of them and I'm writing on one of them right now. The books always hold up Apple as a shining example. An example of hope and rightly so. However, I think there's something missing. If Apple is a great example and the experts have nailed down the reason for their success correctly, then why has no-one been able to replicate even a fraction of that success? Have the reasons for Apple's success not been identified, or is it something that cannot be copied? I think the answer is both.

Here is what I believe. If we look back to when we discussed those special people who make innovation ten times more effective, we get a clue as to Apple's secret sauce. Remember those people had to be creative individuals, dominant in NT characteristics, according to the Myers Briggs test. The key was to take a highly creative person and drum business skills into them, so that they learn to select the best ideas and morph them into something even better.

Now let's look at Steve Jobs' career. Most agree that he had the NT dominance trait. He started a company and was booted out of it for not having the business skills needed. In fact, it's well known that the right CEO for a startup is a very different person to the right CEO for an established company. Generally, you do need to change leadership during the evolution of the company. The Founder's Dilemma, published in the Harvard Business Review, showed that four out of five founders are forced to step down as CEO. Steve Jobs is mentioned as just about the only CEO in history to successfully transition from founder to CEO of a large corporation. But that's not the whole story, is it? He did run the startup well but then was thrown out of his own company, because, at that time, he didn't have the skills to run the established company he had just created. It was probably the right move to oust him.

Being smart and highly resilient, he went off and had a crash course in developing business skills. I can imagine that it was a terrible, stressful time for him but I know from my own life, that those are the times that force you to grow. With his NeXT and Pixar experiences under his belt, he returned with a new skill set. I would argue he was an NT personality that was forced to acquire business skills and that formed him into a Rainmaker^{SM} in the terminology of WinOvations Inc. Of course normally, such a person would never make it to the CEO position but there he was, with the ability to pick the right ideas to back and then help craft them to become even better. Also, think about the importance of the much touted "Champion". Every book says the key to success is to have a Champion in senior management who can help you push ideas forward. It's very rare to find such a champion but Steve didn't need one. He was his own Champion! As CEO, he could make it happen without all the usual roadblocks. It's a wonderfully powerful combination leading to the incredible results we are all very much aware of.

He changed the world. That's what I think happened and it's why it's very hard to copy. It's also why, I am convinced that

Apple is going to gradually slide back into the pool of mediocrity because, believe it or not, that one man was what made the difference. I think that corporations are frightened to admit that one person can make that much difference. It makes them feel vulnerable. Until companies can face up to that reality, they will not be able to recreate the success Apple enjoyed.

I was just reading reviews of a famous book where they had interviewed Steve Jobs and other innovators to uncover their secrets. Of course, this has been attempted over and over again and it has failed every time. If it had succeeded, we would see innovation everywhere, but we don't. Why can't the innovators tell you their secret? It's because what a person does innately is so natural that they don't themselves know what they are doing, or how. I know that first hand because I have always been one of those very creative people and if you were to ask me to describe the process, I would struggle to explain it. I have friends who are extremely likeable with amazing interpersonal skills and yet they claim they are just "regular Joes" who are nothing special. From my perspective, I see that they are special because they exude likeability. I appreciate their affability and the valuable ability to make people want to be around them. It would appear that none of us can truly appreciate and understand our own strengths.

Of course, the goal of interviewing creative types is to identify the mysterious process they use and to replicate it. There is a whole industry selling creativity tools, books and workshops. I believe that it is a waste of time and money. It has been shown that creativity is genetic, so you can't make someone creative. You need to be born with the creativity gene combination and then like anything, practice like heck. You have to be passionate and collect all kinds of information. To us creative types, it's not "just a job". It's an unquenchable thirst for knowledge and creation. The appendix talks more about being an innovator.

When I made a coffee last week with my French press (cafetière), I was frustrated that the second cup had become too strong and bitter. So I thought of a way to improve the design, ordered what I needed and within two days had an improved version with almost no work and minimal cost. Now I can enjoy my second cup. A few months ago, I was annoyed with my gutters acting like drums when the rain hit the horizontal sections, so I looked online for a suitable sound control product. When I found there was no such product on the market, I invented a solution and installed it. Now I can barely hear the gutters when it rains. This is a snapshot of the life of someone who has an insatiable appetite for creating new products. However, like any creative activity, you have spells of high performance and lulls. It's not a systematic process where you can guarantee instant results at any given moment.

Rainmaker is a serial mark of WinOvations Inc.

PROJECTS

Introduction

Projects are held back by several factors and we will discuss each of them. The biggest single issue, is the irrational belief that one can impose a structure on a creative process, with the goals of making it easier to manage and more replicable. Thus the infamous stage-gate (or phase-gate) processes have flourished. We will look at the consequences of that.

Before a formal project can start, a business case is often required. Many companies require a business case even before the pre-study. However, a business case cannot make sense at that stage because there are too many unknowns. Why waste months of time and significant money on a business case before you've checked to see whether the idea has any technical merit or market potential? A pre-study could be done in half the time and using half the money compared to a business case.

It should also be obvious that a business case, by its very nature would turn out negative for any breakthrough product. What would a business case have looked like for the first mp3 player? A manager would have asked "what's the market for an mp3 player?" Answer: "the market size is presently zero". Same answer for the Post-it® Note before it was invented. Project denied, end of story. Business cases cannot work for anything truly new. A company insisting on a positive business case outcome before starting work is doomed to failure in the long-term because they will miss every opportunity for a breakthrough.

43

More Haste, Less Waste

Projects often involve two or more parties, especially as, over the years, companies have tried to push the development work to their suppliers, in order to save money. In other instances, it is the complexity of the new product that necessitates partnership. Either way, one of the first steps is often a non-disclosure agreement (NDA) to allow the parties to communicate freely. I don't know how many such agreements I have signed over the years but I would not be surprised if it was over a hundred. They are often just two pages and contain standard clauses. Somehow every company manages to have a slightly different one. Apparently the lawyers enjoy charging a thousand times for the same product and why wouldn't they, if we let them get away with it?

Anyway, back to the point. These NDAs are an essential part of many projects and all progress is stalled until an agreement is signed. In my experience, this often causes a significant delay. I have twice had major companies ask for an NDA and then take over two years to sign their own, unmodified NDA document. It's unbelievable isn't it? Many companies take several weeks or months. It's a needless delay and it's a sign that there is no sense of urgency at the company, which is even more worrying…but more on that later.

Here are my recommendations. First, ask yourself whether an NDA is really needed. Often you don't need one and can get started by sharing non-confidential information only. When you do need an NDA, it can be accomplished in as little as an hour because the form is standard and you sign the pdf and send it right back via email. Done. If you're a small company dealing with a larger one, try to sign their standard NDA if you can because getting them to make changes will be somewhere between tedious and impossible.

I recently saw a Fortune 50 company execute a three way NDA in about a week. That is stellar performance. On the wall of shame are two Fortune 500 companies who each took over two years to sign their own, unmodified NDAs. Another was pretty bad at six months. In my experience, speed at getting an NDA in place is a good indicator of the overall drive and innovation ability of the company. After all, if you are too lazy to take the first step of a journey, you're probably not going to be winning any races.

Did you know that large companies pay for a service that calls their switchboard to test how many rings it takes to answer and then to monitor the performance of the operators? Perhaps they should consider monitoring their other functions too. If it takes over a month to do a standard NDA, then something is very wrong. Strange that companies are keen to implement control systems like Stage Gate that don't work and yet never check to see whether other functions such as HR or Legal are awake.

There are other procedures that suck the momentum out of your projects, demoralize your project leaders and make your company uncompetitive. Delays occur when a company asks to obtain samples for evaluation. For example, I have worked in mineral companies and clients often ask for a 1 lb sample, which are normally provided free of charge, to speed up the process and as a gesture of goodwill. Several times I have then been asked to complete a multi-page supplier set-up form at this stage. It's an inexcusable waste of my time and theirs to do paperwork to be set up as a vendor when nothing has been sold. However, the mindless paper pushers don't see it that way. Normally, I have been able to reach someone that sees it's inappropriate to set up a new vendor before they have even tested the material, let alone decided to start ordering commercial amounts. This is another topic that can easily be addressed by management. Check your procedures to make sure they are reasonable. The more paperwork your company generates, the less competitive you are. You should view every procedure as a tax on your effectiveness and profitability. They slow you down and huge amounts are spent administering procedures that bring little to no value. If left unmonitored, your people will add more needless work every year. Every time you consider a new procedure, look at how much time it will take. Perhaps you think this is a non-issue, so let me share one of my experiences.

Our network was down and according to ISO 9001, you are not allowed to keep a local copy of any forms on your own computer. You have to get them directly from the server to be 100% sure that you are getting the latest, approved version. I was going away on a business trip and had orders piling up but no-one could access the forms. I wanted to have the orders processed before leaving for my trip, so I processed over ten orders totaling well over $100 000, using the old version of the forms, that had been changed just the week prior. I wanted to be sure that the customers would not get their orders late. The processing lady refused to process the orders. I asked her nicely to please process the orders. She refused. I asked again. She refused again. At that point I was getting annoyed. I pointed out that we were not playing a game, that our salaries and the success of the company depended on making money by selling product. In desperation, I copied some managers hoping for backup but received no support.

Eventually, our own manager came back from a trip and sat us down to resolve the conflict. My colleagues warned me that there was zero chance he would take a stand and help. Her position was that procedures must be followed no matter what. My position was that there has to be a way to process orders even when there are computer issues. I asked him how it was when he first opened the US office. Did he start out with a pile of forms or was the business created without them? Of course, the business had been built up from scratch without any need for forms. I then read out the revision list to show what had been changed when the form was updated. What were the changes that made the old forms, valid until the week prior, completely unacceptable? Can you guess what the change was that was holding up over $100 000 in sales? They had changed the font. Incredible. To everyone's surprise, she was instructed to process the orders on the old form immediately and not to go home until they were all done. She reported me to head office though. Companies are so focused on creating and following procedures that they have lost sight of the big picture. Companies exist to make money not to create unproductive rules. People are paid to do actual work, not to create paperwork.

As I am putting the finishing touches on this book, I have just been exposed to a great example of corporate feebleness. A household name company contacted me for assistance. They had searched all over for a special product they needed for a new event. Even though they had their own sourcing department, they had failed to locate the product and asked me to look on their behalf. It sounded a bit tricky, so I said that I would have to check before accepting the job. An hour or two

47

later I had the answer ready for them and told them so right away. The client said that was great but before we could go further we would need, you guessed it, an NDA. I have no idea why, as there was no need to exchange any secret information but their legal people get their jollies by insisting on procedures. So, we did the NDA in a timely manner. Next he said he would need an official proposal with scope, dates and so on. That seemed a bit much work for a two hour job, where all I needed to do was send him a link to a site selling his specified product. I offered to send him the information right away to save time and trust him to work out the payment later. He thanked me but said that was impossible.

I wrote the proposal and sent it. They immediately wrote back to say they could not accept it without an NDA in place, so my contact had to remind his people that we'd already done that. The ball was now in the court of Purchasing to issue me a purchase order.

We waited two weeks and nothing had happened so he called them and Purchasing had dropped the ball. They then asked for changes to my one page proposal (amazing, I know) and I did them in ten minutes. A day went by and I received an invitation to get set up in their supplier portal. Actually, I received two invitations, each with different passwords, within 30 minutes of each other. I picked one of the two and clicked the link to their portal. My browser said it was unsafe because their certificate was invalid. I tried another browser and it said the same. Imagine that. A Fortune 100 company that insists every supplier uses a secure website where you input all your confidential bank and tax data and the site is insecure. I was told to call the support hotline but no-one picked up.

At that point, I had no choice but to manually override the browser security warning, go to their insecure site and get set up. It is now some days later and I am still waiting to hear from them about the purchase order.

Let's review. I found their solution in a couple of hours and now, because they have invented layers of corporate red tape, a month has passed and I still have not been given the go-ahead to tell them the answer. As I marvel at the incompetence of the company, I wonder whether the executives know about this stuff. It's a very effective job creation scheme but it is not good for the company, the shareholders or us consultants. Companies should not require a consultant doing a two hour, one-off job, to be set up in the same system as a supplier who sells them millions worth of products and services on an ongoing basis.

For a similar sized job, one of the other Fortune 100 companies simply paid me a couple of thousand on their corporate card and I thought "thank goodness, they have some common sense". Since then though, that company changed their rules and paying by card is now a fireable offence. Instead, they have a giant procedure with webinars you have to watch and 90 day payment terms. I support my family with that income. I do not want to jump through hoops, like a performing seal and then wait a quarter of a year to get paid.

Here are some thoughts. Stop making it impossible for your people to do their jobs. Stop making it impossible for consultants to help you. Find someone with common sense and send them out into your company to document all the insane procedures that have built up and make recommendations on how you can get back to doing real work.

STAGE-GATE MEANS LONG WAIT

"When you do not know what you are doing, do it neatly, efficiently, and decisively."
anon (Guidelines for Successful Planners)

What is Stage-Gate or Phase-Gate? It is a system for project management which is claimed to help you with your innovation process by introducing structure. That sounds excellent in theory. Apparently people buy the idea, literally, because 80% of the Fortune 500 use it. They each paid up for a virtually identical system to help them structure their efforts. You would think that, with that amount of money spent, it must be very effective and well proven. So, what do you find when you look at innovation project effectiveness over the last few decades, as Stage-Gate has swept the market? We find that instead of an improvement, the launch rate for successful new products has actually declined. That means that a lot of money has been spent on software and manuals only to get worse results. Even more money has been spent on training, data input, meetings and tracking. All for nothing, or, actually, less than nothing, i.e. negative results. Here are the findings on the effectiveness of Stage-Gate...

"Even as the use of stage-gate NBD processes within major corporations has grown to now exceed 75%, the average percentage of products new to the company in the preceding five years has declined from 32% to 28% in the last ten years. At the very least, traditional linear stage-gate NBD processes are not working well enough. Could the "cure" (standard linear stage-gate NBD processes) be even worse than the disease?"

"The challenge is that in the 50 years or so since they were first developed, conversion rates of ideas into successful launches have maintained steady at a very low level and that in fact organisations that use stage-gate processes are no more effective than organisations which have no process at all (Stevens and Burley, 2003)."

We used a version of it when I worked at Electrolux (Frigidaire to Americans), one of the world's largest manufacturers of household appliances. It was very effective at making you spend lots of time on administration instead of focusing on the actual project. They paid for a fancy manual and system called IPDP which consisted of Phase-Gates. They created two separate custom databases in Lotus Notes to track it all. When the meetings came to decide the fate of a project, they took forever to schedule because the people were senior and busy. The project could be on hold for one or two months waiting for the next meeting. Then, when the meetings came, we proudly presented our progress and waited for the green, orange or red light. The meeting ended and no decision was made. Everyone shuffled out without a word. Apparently we in R&D were expected to follow the system but no-one in management knew their role was to make a decision. So, in the absence of direction, we just continued on.

I recently spoke to someone at Bostik who said that "introduction of Stage-Gate had doubled their administration work". In fact, I have never spoken to anyone experienced in running technical projects that thought Stage-Gate was a good use of time. As we have seen, the studies have conclusively proven that it is indeed a waste of time. Experienced project managers recommend bypassing the process and some books do too. If you want to tell the difference between a real innovator and a pretend one, then ask them for their view on Stage-Gate. If they advocate for it, then you can be almost certain that they have no actual experience of innovation. Brutal maybe, but true.

If that is the case, then why is it so popular? I can tell you why. Managers at large companies are uncomfortable with innovation. It's an unpredictable, creative process that they can't control and that scares them. Large companies are like the military in that they rely on structure to give stability. Creativity is the opposite of that. It's the unknown and it is human nature to fear the unknown. Furthermore, we have to think about personality types. Some types of people prefer tools and systems and that type of person often ends up in management. I recently saw a CFO promoted to CEO. A CFO likes tools and systems to control everything. You can sell them a Stage-Gate process (that doesn't work), an SAP® system (that likely cripples your company while it's implemented), a CRM system (that has your sales people doing busy-work instead of selling) and so on. There is a perception that putting a CFO in charge is a safe choice. While they may help maintain a "steady as she goes" approach which works in the short term, the long term consequence is likely to be very detrimental. Tools are very valuable for orderly, predictable processes but utterly counterproductive for creative, disordered ones.

> *"Order is the antithesis of creativity."*
> Chris DeArmitt

Search online for "The Dyneema® Project" and read Romancing the Thread: the Story of Dyneema® to see an example of how breakthrough innovation actually takes place in the real world. As you will see, it's a tale of delay and management negativity overcome by bravery and rule breaking. That's what it takes to create a revolutionary product. It's about breaking the system, the exact opposite of Stage-Gate. Speak to any successful creator in a large company and they will tell you they have learned how to get around the system in order to make progress.

Here's an example from my time at Electrolux / Frigidaire. As I mentioned, we ran a Phase-Gate system at Electrolux with all the admin and slow-down that brings. In my four years there, I recall just one truly innovative product that was released. That was the Trilobite vacuum cleaner launched in 2001. You can read about it and see a picture of it on Wikipedia. It was the first small robotic, fully automated vacuum cleaner. It would work out the shape of your room and then walk around continuously vacuuming at low power to keep it clean. Then it would dock and recharge as needed. You can see commercials for similar products on TV now but back then it was revolutionary. Surely this must be a shining example of big company innovation delivered using their wonderful, expensive Phase-Gate process! Not quite. Read on...

The Trilobite project was run according to Phase-Gate, all our projects were. However, it was stopped every time a decision point was reached. Why? Electrolux made standard, relatively inexpensive vacuum cleaners and this high-tech product didn't fit at all in their product range. Plus, it was incredibly complicated and unproven, bringing up reliability concerns. So every time a decision point came, they cancelled the project and for sound reasons. Then a strange thing happened. At a company party, a senior executive asked about the project and how it was progressing. The next day the team started work again so they would have something to report to him. That's

53

how the project was resurrected, more than once, and eventually reached the working prototype stage. They made something like 13 and 10 of them died tumbling down stairs. Things didn't look too encouraging because the sensor system couldn't detect stairs. However, the product was certainly the coolest thing they were working on and looked the coolest too. So they proudly showed the press and it was even featured on a BBC TV show way back in 1996.

Years went by and they kept showing the prototypes to the press but it was no closer to commercialization. Then something odd happened. There was an article in a Swedish newspaper saying that Electrolux had only used the Trilobite to get free media attention and had no intention to sell it. Of course that was true. Another newspaper followed with a similar article, stating that Electrolux has taken advantage of the media and should be ashamed. Right again. So, Electrolux went ahead and launched the product out of shame. A product that was over five times the cost of their other offerings, had questionable reliability and a lemming-like propensity to throw itself off cliffs, sorry, I meant stairs.

This is how products actually come to market. Here we saw the power of a Champion. In this case the influence of the Champion was enough to get the product validated and to the end of the Stage-Gate process, even though it made no sense. His influence was not enough to make it go commercial. Champions are very powerful but must be able to tell the difference between worthwhile product ideas and duds.

In the 1990s, Motorola formed a company to create the Iridium satellite system allowing phone access even in remote locations. The story is that a senior champion pushed it through because he believed in it. However, it turned out to make no sense. It demanded enormous investment and although it worked around the whole globe, it demanded line of sight to the 66 satellites. Thus, it would not work inside buildings or cars. It was good for people in remote locations where cell service was not yet available but the population in those regions was too low, and the people too poor, to support the expensive service. In 1999, they filed for bankruptcy and defaulted on $1.5BN of debt. The fiasco was listed by Time magazine as one of the "The 10 Biggest Tech Failures of the Last Decade". Interestingly, that system is still in use today and there are plans to update it. This may be an example of a good idea that was executed too early. Sometimes that happens.

The person who invented the SLR camera had that same problem. He showed his revolutionary design to the camera producers and they agreed that it was excellent. There was just one problem. At that time, it was impossible to manufacture the specially shaped prism upon which it was based. The unfortunate inventor was too far ahead of his time and didn't live to see his invention adopted globally in later years.

I have spoken to some of the people I respect most and the general opinion is that some kind of light structure is fine for innovation. Checklists can be used to ensure all is in order and you can call meetings to review progress. However, it should be run as a non-cumbersome system that keeps the momentum flowing, instead of the full system which saps energy and grinds progress to a halt. To be honest, if you have hired competent project managers, they will not forget anything critical to success. The approach of large companies appears to be to hire whoever is least expensive and then put systems in place to prevent them from making a mess of everything. Smaller companies hire as if every hire were critical, because every hire is critical.

The good news is that you can remove Stage-Gate, save tons on software and admin and make your projects go faster at the same time. Creative people hate admin work, so you'll be more likely to attract and keep them if you eliminate the tedium. It's obvious why we wouldn't want to spend money on a system that costs money and robs us of time by imposing unneeded administrative burden. But why is it so important not to slow down the process? Slowing down new product creation has a chain reaction effect which spirals out of control. People tend to stay in their position for only a couple of years. I have been involved in three year projects where the project leader left and was replaced several times. At best, there was always a significant delay as the new person became familiar with the status of the work. At worst, the new project leader abandoned all prior progress and started again from the beginning because they had their own convictions about the best way to proceed. This musical chairs effect is not limited to the project leader. In a project life there will be a personnel turnover that increases exponentially the longer the project runs. It is therefore essential to run a few projects quickly rather than run more projects slowly.

On the opposite side of the coin, there is a knock-on positive effect when running a few fast projects that do come to fruition. It creates a rewarding experience for all involved, so the workers are energized and motivated for the next challenge. Likewise, management see results and are then inclined to support the next project. Remember that the managers don't expect to be in their position for more than a couple of years either. Therefore, they are incentivized only to support quick projects that can make them look good and get them promoted.

Stage-Gate and Six Sigma are example of corporation leaders' fanaticism for implementation of control systems without first checking whether they actually work. These, presumably smart, people are paid wild sums of money to lead companies with insight and strategy. Instead they try to put the company on auto-pilot by using fancy control systems, that don't actually work.

ACROSS THE BORDER

I was born in the USA and grew up in England. After my PhD, I moved to Stockholm Sweden where I worked for about 9 years in R&D, first as a post-doc at the KTH University, then at the Institute for Surface Chemistry as group leader. I then made my move to industry to work at the central R&D for Electrolux, they had 80 000 employees at that time and were the world's largest manufacturer of household appliances. As described elsewhere in the book, they closed that whole R&D facility and I moved to Italy for a year and worked, still in R&D at a gigantic washing machine factory. Next I went to Germany to be with my then girlfriend, now wife, Anna. I applied to BASF's HQ in Ludwigshafen and was offered a job in marketing which was a new experience for me. The last several years have been spent working in the USA for smaller companies as Chief Scientist, CTO and so on. Those latter roles involved a combination of technical, marketing and sales skills. I have also run my own consulting company Phantom Plastics LLC for several years.

I mention all that to explain that it's been a rather diverse career spanning all kinds of company size, job function and country. It has given some perspective on how innovation works in different countries and I thought you might be interested to get some views and tips. My happiest times were probably in Sweden, partly because the Swedes, as a whole, are exceptionally honest and that's a quality that is very important to me.

There is more to be learnt from inter-country differences. I learnt something extremely interesting and useful from my good friend Robert Huber at BASF. You may not realize this, but one of the main factors slowing innovation in conservative countries like the USA, the UK, Germany etc. is that they are risk averse. You can get your project through the early stages and then you will hit a wall because you cannot get an opening to test it in full scale production at the factory. I struggled with that when at Electrolux and later at BASF. After all, a factory makes money when they are producing product and running trials means lost productivity and less profit. So you find that it is very hard to get that crucial verification that your new process, or product, will run in a full production environment. At Electrolux, there was a shut-down at Christmas time when they would do maintenance. To get a trial done, you pretty much had to wait until that time every year. They would have to run the machines extra hard to build inventory in advance, to make up for the lost production during the trial. Then, if the stars were aligned just right, you got your all-important factory trial. If something went wrong, then you could be forced to wait for the next chance, maybe in the summer, or the following Christmas. Amazing, I know, but remember, the production manager gets his bonus based on productivity, so what's his incentive to help out? This actually ties into the famous Champion idea. In order to make a factory manager help you, your Champion would have to be senior to the factory manager. That's why you need a Champion who is very high up indeed.

So, Robert had a special product he wanted to sell and was not able to get factory trials at his potential customers. They basically said, we're busy manufacturing, come back when you can prove to us that it works. They would rather follow than lead. Faced with that message and being a resourceful,

59

tenacious chap, Robert decided to find a way around the road block. He went on a trip to Mexico where he was able to run five factory trials at five different companies in one week. He came back with all the information needed to convince the Germans to proceed and give his product an evaluation. I thought it was pure genius of him to use cultural differences to his advantage. He went to a country where change is welcomed, where they are hungry for change. I would encourage others to use this method to dramatically accelerate commercialization.

RISK AND REWARD

"In any great organization it is far, far safer to be wrong with the majority than to be right alone."
John Kenneth Galbraith

Several times in my career I have been inside companies demanding innovation, with the CEO imploring us to deliver it. It's easy for them to ask for innovation but where is the support? Do they not realize that the person trying to push through something new is putting themselves at risk? So, what is the reward for that risk? Let's say you somehow succeed and create a new blockbuster product, like the famous 3M Post-It® Note. What would you get for it? Do you receive a life-sized bronze statue, a million dollar bonus and a lifelong employment contract? I checked and the people who invented the Post-It® received no extra payment whatsoever.

"Neither Art Fry nor Spencer Silver received any special financial compensation from 3M for their achievements, but both continued to work at the company and invent new products. In 1984, Fry was promoted to division scientist. In 1986, he was promoted to corporate scientist, the highest designation an employee can achieve on the technical side of the 3M corporate ladder. In 1985, Time magazine declared Post-it® Notes one of the best products of the previous twenty-five years."

To me, that is not only incredible, but incredibly unjust. They made a money printing press for the company and yet received no reward.

Is that an isolated incident? I checked on the person who is attributed with inventing the internet. He received nothing for 20 years and then, as an afterthought, he got a small prize. Luckily, he was still alive to receive it. In interviews he's described as wistful and somewhat bitter. I would be too. How would you feel if you'd invented the internet and were reminded every week that you had changed the world and yet somehow not made any money out of it? I'd feel like the world's biggest sucker.

What about the man who invented cyanoacrylate glue (known as Krazy Glue®, Super Glue® and many other names) which instantly glues not only plastics, wood, ceramics and metal but is also used to seal wounds? His name was Dr. Harry Coover. Despite the tremendous amount of money the invention made for several companies and its usefulness to society, he did not become wealthy from it. The companies involved took so long to make it a commercial success that the patents had expired by then. He did eventually get an award from President Obama shortly before his death. When are we going to start paying the inventors who changed the world instead of giving them a medal on their deathbed?

Another great inventor, James West, co-invented the electret microphone which revolutionized the industry making up 90% of all microphones produced today. They are in every cell phone for example. He worked at Bell Labs and retired with over 200 patents to his name. Here is what is written about him.

"Over the years, West says, he earned only $1 from all the patents that bear his name. As members of the Bell Labs research team, scientists like West did not personally profit from their inventions."

What a shocking rip off.

As I'm a plastics and materials expert, it's natural for me to check examples I know about from those fields. Everyone has heard of Kevlar, an amazingly strong type of nylon that is most famous for use in bullet proof vests and cut resistant gloves. Over a million such vests have been sold so far. It is an invention so important that it has changed the lives of many and saved the lives of some. Recently, Stefanie Kwolek, the inventor of Kevlar, died and I checked the ensuing articles to see how she was rewarded for her work. This is what I found in an article in the New York Times just after her death.

"Its popularity has proved a windfall for DuPont. Kevlar has generated several billion dollars in revenue for the company. Ms. Kwolek did not directly benefit from it financially, however; she signed over patent royalties to DuPont."

So, she made billions for DuPont and received nothing.

I have seen the same sad story first hand. I worked at BASF's headquarters in Ludwigshafen Germany. It's a gigantic factory with over 30 000 employees on that one site alone. Having come from an R&D background, they put me in marketing because that's the normal career path at BASF. I learned a lot and enjoyed the new perspective. What I saw was that the marketing people had been asking for solutions from R&D and not getting them, so I moved to R&D to have a go at fixing that. I did some work I'm proud of and several patents resulted. One instance was when a customer requested a plastic that was cloudy at room temperature but would become clear when heated. It then had to return to cloudy when cooled back down to room temperature. No such plastic existed and I was out on a business trip when the request came to me. I called in four formulations to try and one of them turned transparent at just the right temperature i.e. 65°C. We had the new material made, tested and ready to go in just eight days from the customer request. I proudly told a manager who joked, "great, now we will expect you to complete every project in eight days". What was my reward? Nothing of course. Creation of a brand new smart plastic in eight days. It's patented and you can see it in operation on my website where a video shows it changing from milky to clear when heated. I have had interest from many major companies all around the world. They want it for everything from toys to windows that automatically block heat when it's too hot and sunny.

Other work I am rather proud of, was also done during my BASF days. They had been wrestling with a problem for 30 years. It was a serious quality issue related to a plastic they sell in the hundreds of thousands of tons per year. My good friend Dr. Graham McKee told me that quality problem had plagued them for decades and said they had spent probably three million Euros on it. The problem was so famous, even the chairman of the board, Juergen Hambrecht knew about it. One senior manager described it as the "Sword of Damocles". He said that the customers held it over their heads in negotiations and used it to drive down the price.

Scores of PhD chemists had taken a crack at it and they had all failed. I saw proof when I entered my new office in R&D and spotted a bookshelf three feet wide literally packed with reports detailing all of those failed attempts. I shared an office with Dr.

Michael Ishaque, who became a good friend. He had just been working on the infamous problem and he explained why the challenge was, in his view, fundamentally impossible to solve. His explanation was valuable because understanding a problem properly is crucial and he laid it out perfectly. I told him that I didn't agree that it was impossible and started to mull over concepts. Some weeks later, when I was about to leave for a holiday, I realized I'd better leave some work for my technicians to do while I was gone. So, I wrote down five ideas to try on a sheet of paper and off I went for one of those long vacations you can take in Europe because you get lots of vacation there.

I came back three weeks later and my technician, a wonderful man called Alexander Ludwig, told me that the first idea had worked. I was surprised and excited, so I asked him to do it again to make sure. After so many years of dashed hopes, I would have to be 100% sure before I would dare tell anyone. So, he successfully repeated the work and I went next door to tell my friend Graham. I still remember his words. He said "lock the door and we will write the patent right now, otherwise every manager in BASF will try to get his name on it". In Germany you get royalties for your patents, so being listed as an inventor means cash and this patent had the potential to become a super valuable one. When you look at a BASF patent you can be almost certain to find names of people on there who didn't contribute in any way to the invention. They are the names of managers who insisted on being added as an inventor, so that they could get a share of the patent royalties. Shockingly, in our department we were also under orders not to list our technicians as inventors, even when they had actually done some of the inventing.

Anyway, I did lock the door and we wrote that patent. The managers were amazed to find that someone had solved the famous problem. The R&D department head grudgingly admitted how clever the solution was. We went on and scaled it up on the pilot plant. Then we showed that it worked perfectly in full scale production at the factory, which is a big deal. It was a cheap, safe and easy to implement solution. A very tough and rare combination to achieve.

We were talking about risk and reward. What did I get for this monumental achievement? I solved the longest standing, most famous problem there was. I did it on my own initiative and without any funding, nor a running project. The department head promised me a promotion to the next salary band. Promotion time came and nothing happened, so I asked him about it. He said that he had put my name forward but the business unit head had blocked it. I found that a bit surprising as the business unit head was far above me and hardly knew of my existence, so I didn't know how I could have offended him. So, I asked to meet him and find out why he had blocked my promotion. He said my name was never on the promotion list and he certainly had not blocked it. The business unit head was not pleased that the department head had used his name in the deception. I assume they met and discussed it because next thing I knew the department head called me to a meeting to evaluate my performance. I thought that was odd because it was the wrong time of year for evaluations. So in I went and he explained that I was useless and was doing a terrible job. He handed me an evaluation form full of D grades and I said "that's very funny, you should have your own comedy show on TV".

And that's why I left BASF.

"It is not the business of authority figures to validate genius, because genius threatens authority."
Gordon MacKenzie from Orbiting the Giant Hairball

I put my technician Alex up for a one-time bonus for his outstanding work on that project. It was approved by my boss but it never came, so I asked what had happened. I was told that the department head said he had "lost the paperwork and maybe he would pay it next year". I went ballistic. I went to personnel and they agreed that it should rightly be paid, but it still was not. I wrote an email explaining that I was going to go one level higher every week until it was paid. I would go to the business unit head, then to the board member for our division and then the chairman of the board of BASF. That threat got him his token bonus. Apparently, those are the lengths you have to go to in order to get what's right and what had been promised. My managers wouldn't do it for me, but I believe in doing what's right, no matter what. Unfortunately, it places me in a small minority and gets me into trouble sometimes.

"Even if you are a minority of one, the truth is the truth."
Mahatma Gandhi

Funnily enough, someone in another division offered me a promotion shortly thereafter, but by then, I had seen enough of their incompetent management and lack of ethics. It's a pity because I gave BASF every bit of effort and creativity I had and all I got was empty promises and persecution. I stay in touch with the many good friends I made there and I miss those long, long, holidays.

My friend Graham, who had 210 patents, earned just ten percent extra salary from royalties but at least he got something. In other countries you get no royalties. Some people will only have one really good idea that gets commercialized in their whole career. In that case, they just blew their one big chance at security for themselves and their family, for nothing in return.

It seems that after millions of years, we are now attempting to reverse Darwinian evolution. What do I mean by that? If you are inept enough to spill hot coffee on yourself, by all means collect a million dollar reward. On the other hand, if you invent something that changes the world for the better you may collect $1 for your patent. Something has gone very wrong.

You have probably heard examples of the inventor becoming rich and indeed that is possible. How do they do it? The man who invented the bar code waited while it was adopted world-wide and said not a word about his patent. Once is was ubiquitous, he then enforced his patent and began collecting huge settlements from the automotive industry, the household appliance industry and so on. His estate made a fortune. I was at Electrolux when they collected a million from us. Had he asked for a license fee from the beginning, it probably would not have taken off as it did because companies don't like to pay for anything, if they can help it. He was clever and waited until huge investments had been made and it was too late for companies to back out. They had come to rely on barcodes. I read that the jpg image format was also allowed to proliferate for years, followed by attempts to enforce patents on the technology. Becoming wealthy from your invention is the rare exception and requires cunning tactics.

Let's recap on the innovators risk versus reward balance in a corporation. You are being asked to rock the boat and drive something through from the bottom of the organization with no support, risking your job and your reputation. Now, that's risk! So what's the reward? As we just heard, you can expect somewhere between zero and a small one-time bonus. Earlier we mentioned the study at Dow showing that when it was time to lay off employees, the non creative types were all kept whereas 50% of the Myers Briggs NT type difference makers were let go. Why? Because although the companies scream for innovation, when you try to deliver change they get irritated and fire you to preserve the easy life. It's happened to me. I read an amusing piece of advice online just last week. It said that if none of your R&D team has ever been fired in their career then you don't have any true innovators. It's an interesting observation but why should the people trying hardest to help you be punished? It turns out that big companies are a popularity contest. Smile a lot and suck up to your manager if you want to do well. We now know that the innovator's dilemma is whether to bravely attempt innovation for zero reward and possible termination, or to abandon their dreams and play it safe.

"You have enemies? Good. That means you've stood up for something, sometime in your life."
                                                    Winston Churchill

THE COMPANY

INTRODUCTION

"We find everywhere a type of organization (administrative, commercial, or academic) in which the higher officials are plodding and dull, those less senior are active only in intrigue against each other, and the junior men are frustrated or frivolous."

C. Northrup Parkinson

He made those observations in his famous 1957 book entitled Parkinson's Law and I have seen no evidence of change in the time that has elapsed since.

Innovation is performed largely within the confines of a company. The company is the setting or framework and as such, plays an important role. It can help you, or hinder you, depending on how well it is set up. Therefore, we will now look at the various company functions that can impact attempts at innovation.

HR: Human Resources or Holiday Resort?

"If you hire mediocre people, they will hire mediocre people."
Tom Murphy

Big companies are mediocrity magnets. By definition, the larger the sample, the more it tends toward a standard bell curve distribution. That's statistics, or probability. When I worked at BASF they thought that they were the best but in reality they were not any better than the mean. In some ways they were worse due to a degree of arrogance, leading to complacency.

Who or what is responsible for the indifferent quality of staff? In many large, well-respected companies, HR have delegated their job to computers via the dreaded Taleo®. I have vowed never to work for any company that uses Taleo® or BrassRing because it is a sign that leadership have checked out. They clearly give not one whit for the quality of their staff.

Years ago, I was approached about a job at Invista™ (part of Koch Industries). We had some discussions and they decided to proceed and get me in for a formal interview. They said they would have to follow procedures and have me apply online through, you guessed it, Taleo®. They created a job opening so I could apply and sent me the link. I applied and within 5 minutes received an automatically generated email from Taleo® telling me that I was not suitable for the role. Just think about that for

74

a moment. I was rejected for a job posting they had created specifically for me. That is what happens when our applications are evaluated by a computer system. If this were a normal job posting, I would have had no recourse. In this case, I was able to contact the hiring people and they rewrote the job description so that I would pass.

You might think I'm being too harsh on HR, but I'm pretty convinced because the views are based on many experiences over some decades. My wife was looking for a job and heard nothing back after making many applications for jobs she was well qualified for. Eventually, she was called for interview and hired. Her new boss told her that she had not even received my wife's résumé from HR. Instead she had walked to HR, in another building, and manually sorted through the résumés that HR had collected and abandoned in a pile. Fortunately for my wife, that proactive boss did HR's job for them. Not every applicant can expect to be that lucky. Do people in HR not care that other people's livelihoods are at stake?

Another friend related a similar story. He saw new graduates from his Alma Mater and asked them why they were not applying to his company. HR had told him that no-one had applied for the open positions. The students said that they had applied. So, he went back to HR and asked where the applications were. HR replied, "oh, here they are." The attitude of HR towards hiring reminds me of a Simpsons episode. Homer takes the day off and someone asks him who is doing his job at the nuclear power plant. Homer says "don't worry, I found someone to cover for me" and the scene cuts to one of those drinking bird toys pecking at the Y key on Homer's keyboard. A nuclear meltdown is the consequence of Homer's abdication of responsibility. Of course when Homer does it, it's funny. It's not so amusing when the HR of major corporations do the same. Do they really think that they can leave a computer program to do their job? Where is their sense of pride or duty? Why is no-one checking to make sure they are actually doing their job? Why are they entrusting such lackluster specimens with the future of the company?

Some years ago, a VP at PolyOne™ approached me about becoming a technology scout for them. The whole process was a disaster and lasted well over a year. At one point I was told by HR that my interview had been postponed because the CEO had died. Then they changed their mind and said he wasn't dead after all. They called me to 2 separate days of interviews over several months with 4 people per interview of whom 6 were VPs. One person told me during my interview "don't come work here if you want to get anything done, you'll just be stuck in meetings all day". A complete stranger told me that. Things must have been bad indeed to compel such a candid outburst. After more than a year of interviews, they decided not to offer me the job. You can imagine the impression that made.

There is another, even more negative consequence of poor hiring. Bad people in a company are very destructive. They create a bad atmosphere, cause a huge drain of money and they can even ruin the careers of others. I've seen it first hand several times. At BASF I took over the lab and technicians of one infamous chap. He had presented impressive results and achieved the much coveted promotion out of R&D to Marketing. That's the typical career path for PhD chemists at BASF. So there I was with his old lab and his former technicians ready to start work on my projects but there was a problem. The product he had created and validated in the lab was being scaled up for production at the factory and it was not going well at all. They desperately needed help, so they took one of my two technicians because he was most familiar with the new product, having helped develop it. They also assigned a very capable senior scientist to assist with the scale-up problems. After two or three months and what must have been a few hundred thousand Euros, it still didn't work. My technician explained why. The technology had never worked in the lab. My predecessor had presented false results to get his promotion and leave the mess to someone else. The poor factory manager was tearing his hair out wondering why his efforts to produce that product were failing. Eventually someone told him that it was not his fault, the whole thing was a scam.

With one technician gone, I was left with one. However, she was sent to help another colleague who had taken over the other project from my infamous predecessor. It wasn't working either. The department head asked the new project leader something like "what's wrong with you? This worked for the guy who was just promoted". Embarrassing for the unfortunate young lady who had been given his former project. So, my technician was sent to help her. The technician tried to replicate the experiment in the same flask and in the same lab that the newly promoted person had used. It didn't work.

A fundamental principle of science is that if you repeat something exactly, then it must work. I asked my technician what was up. She explained that the technology had never worked. My predecessor had made that up too. I felt sorry for the poor lady who had to take over that project. She was unjustly treated like a loser by the manager (the same manager who had lied about my promotion and "lost" my technician's bonus). My predecessor on the other hand faced no consequences for falsifying his work and wasting months of company time and hundreds of thousands of Euros. It sends a powerfully negative message when you stand behind liars and persecute the honest. That's not the kind of company I want to be a part of.

"Somebody once said that in looking for people to hire, you look for three qualities: integrity, intelligence, and energy. And if you don't have the first, the other two will kill you. You think about it; it's true. If you hire somebody without integrity, you really want them to be dumb and lazy."

Warren Buffett

Especially over the last ten years or so, I have been shocked by the lack of honesty at the workplace. I have seen people using a company credit card for tens of thousands of dollars without receipts or approval. Personnel and management didn't care. I have seen people with lies on their résumé. Personnel and management didn't care. I have heard about bribery of customers. Personnel and management didn't care. I have seen people promised bonuses and promotions that never came. No-one cared. I have seen intentional falsification of safety and quality records. Same result. I have seen other things so scary that I don't dare write them here. Until we start hiring ethical people and firing the unethical, companies will not be good places to work and will be crippled by internal friction.

So, if the norm is lackadaisical or downright bad HR, what happens when a company has good HR? That has been studied and the results are impressive.

The Boston Consulting Group (BCG) showed that companies from Fortune Magazine's list of 100 Best Companies to Work For…

"...consistently enjoyed better economic performance than those less capable. In several topics, this correlation was striking—up to 3.5 times the revenue growth and as much as 2.1 times the average profit margin."

In fact, companies who consistently appeared on that list outperformed the S&P 500 by 99 percent over a 10 year period (BCG, From Capability to Profitability: Realizing the Value of People Management).

As I look back over the companies I have interacted with, I was hoping there would be at least one that stood out as having unusually "decent" people, i.e. people with integrity. Eastman Chemical Company is the one that springs to mind. Having met perhaps 20 people from that company over the years, I have been continually impressed with their employees. So much so, that I suspected it was no coincidence. I called someone I know there and sure enough, they have a careful hiring, training and nurturing process in place. Clearly, it works.

In my whole career I only recall having my personality tested once in an interview. Why is it that HR typically makes no effort whatever to work out what kind of person you are and fit you to the job? It helps them and it helps you. Apparently spending a few minutes is too much work. It's a shocking display of laziness and incompetence in my view. In Sweden and several other countries in Europe, it's virtually impossible to fire someone once hired. In that scenario it would be especially prudent to screen the people before being stuck with them for years, or decades. At Dow they spent a couple of years consciously moving people into positions that fit their personality and the results were very positive. They put creative types into fuzzy front end positions, dealing with the early stages of a project and the people good at completing work were assigned to the later stages. They estimated that they needed about 30% creatives and 70% finishers to get the right balance for optimal results.

As a generalization, most HR people seem to think it's their job to fill seats as cheaply as possible. We've all heard that the "employees are our greatest asset" but it sure doesn't seem that way. It seems obvious to me that if you want to outperform the competition, you will need above average staff. We see it in sports every day and we understand it intuitively. So, why aren't companies doing it? Multiplying mediocrity does not create greatness. Here's an analogy: "you can open as many McDonald's restaurants as you want, but it won't win you a star in the Michelin Guide!" In sports, a top star gets compensated accordingly but not so in industry. They will do anything to avoid paying for performance. They will say you can't be paid more than your manager. They will show you a curve of salary versus age and explain why you can't deviate from that.

One of my very close friends and one of the best performers I have ever met, recently had his evaluation. They said that they thought he deserved a raise for his excellent work but would not give him one in order to bring him more in line with the salaries of his colleagues. He has been at the company just a couple of years and had specifically asking during the hiring process whether his starting salary would hold back his progression. He was told that it would not.

When I announced that I would leave Electrolux and move to BASF a friend in HR asked me why. He said they had great plans for me. This was at a party over a glass of wine. I was surprised and asked him why there had been no mention of these plans. If a person is recognized, then tell them what you have planned. Don't wait until they have signed a contract elsewhere.

Why do companies try so extraordinarily hard to make sure that the top performers are paid the same as the ones who, for whatever reason, are not performing? It sends a powerful message. My friend heard the message that there is no future in that company for a hard working person who delivers outstanding results. I am sure he will soon be using his talents somewhere else, where he will, I hope, be appreciated. It actually doesn't cost much to keep a top performer. They may deliver 2-3 times more value than most employees but you can make them happy with only 25-50% extra pay. That's quite a deal. On the other hand, if you don't show them any appreciation, then soon you may find them working for your competition and eating you for breakfast.

Occasionally, the system does work. In my first job (at Cookson in the UK) I was making great progress on a new tableware glaze project. Glaze is the shiny glass layer on your ceramic plates and cups at home. I had a girlfriend in Sweden and went to the Director to resign so I could move abroad. I had tears in my eyes as I resigned and I was ready to refuse any offer of more money. Even doubling my salary would not have worked. However, that director, Steve Bold, carefully listened to what I said, so he understood what had driven my decision. He was silent for a while and then said "so, you want to spend more time with your girlfriend in Sweden". I said "yes". He said "what about some extra holiday?". I was taken aback by the surprise turn of events. It felt like he was a magician who had just pulled a rabbit out of a hat. I asked him how much holiday he had in mind and he said "how about an extra couple of months". Then I really was in shock. That conversation will stay with me forever as an example of compassion and great leadership. I wish I could have stayed and worked for him. He's retired now but I try to stay in touch because he showed me what a classy person he is. It's rare to find someone like that. If you do find a great manager, try to stay with them, if at all possible.

FROM THE TOP

*"The ear of the leader must ring with the
voices of the people."*

Woodrow Wilson

Often new CEOs come in from another industry and don't really understand the details of the business they are now running. Somehow, it is incorrectly assumed that once you've been CEO of one company, you are automatically qualified to lead any other company. Typically, after some months at the job, the new CEO announces a reorganization. If they had been running a matrix organization, they switch to a line organization, or vice versa. The structure itself is irrelevant because the change is really just a proclamation that they are now in charge. Of course, any reorganization paralyses the company, so it is not to be done frivolously.

Eventually the CEO departs, taking a giant golden handshake and leaves it to some person from yet another industry to come in and repeat the same cycle. They can be viewed as politicians who make nice election promises but after a couple of years, it becomes clear there are lackluster results. At that point, the Board looks for a new candidate, with a new line of promises and so the pattern is repeated.

Here's an example of just that pattern. I worked for a company when a new President was announced for the US office. First he met with us all and made specific promises to each of us.

Then a few months later, he took office and immediately broke them all. In his first 8 weeks 50% of the company staff had resigned or been fired. One of them was the sole finance lady who doubled as the head of HR. Three months after she left in disgust they still could not do their financial reporting, had no idea who owed them money, or how much tax they owed. They proceeded to spend a fortune in consultants and airfares trying to work it out. They spent ten times more than it would have cost to keep his promise to give her a modest pay rise.

Is everyone in upper management and HR asleep? Surely an alarm bell should ring when 50% of your key personnel leave in the first two months after a new manager takes over. You may be thinking this was a conscious plan to downsize but it was quite the reverse. The US was a target growth market and they had just spent 100,000 dollars upgrading to a larger office the year prior in preparation for that growth.

Poor management at all levels is holding back innovation. Innovation means risk and these are risk averse people. Innovation takes time. Usually more time than the manager expects to stay in their position. If they can't get any credit for creating the innovation, then why should they foster it? I can see why they rather focus on other easier topics like downsizing and making false promises.

When I was at Electrolux/Frigidaire, Michael Treschow was President for most of my time there. I just looked him up and Wikipedia describes him as follows:

"As chairman of the board of both Unilever since 2007 and the Confederation of Swedish Enterprise, and former chairman of Ericsson, Treschow is one of the most influential people in Swedish business today."

At no stage did he ever share a vision for the company with us, the employees. His contribution was to make one truly pathetic speech every Christmas at the headquarters, where I worked. I was therefore shocked to read in a Swedish newspaper that, in an interview, he said that he'd like to double R&D spending. Needless to say, we in R&D were highly encouraged. Imagine then our emotions when, just two months later, he fired 70% of the R&D staff and closed down the whole of the company's main R&D facility in Stockholm. I wrote him an email asking about the discrepancy between his stated intentions and subsequent actions. To his credit, he did reply. He explained that although he would like to double R&D spending, he could not do so and had decided to make cuts instead. So, he crippled R&D and handed the reigns over to the next chap. Treschow was known as "The Axman" because he just went from one company to the next making layoffs and moving on. From what I saw, any random person picked off the street could have done his job and for a lot less money.

We have seen why short-termism encourages non constructive behavior. What is the right way then? Some years ago, I remember an outcry when the CEO of Disney was getting an enormous payout. Then I heard a radio interview with the details. It explained that he had accepted the job on a very low base salary and with a large amount of stock and options which would only have value if the share price increased by the time they had vested. A person would only accept such an offer if they believed the company had potential and believed that they could deliver results. So, he worked diligently to strengthen the company and lo and behold the company flourished, the shareholders got what they wanted and he became deservedly wealthy. I have no problem with that approach. It's a win for the CEO, a win for the company and a win for the shareholder. Most importantly, for the purposes of this book at least, it encourages long term thinking and a sincere focus on the innovation pipeline.

There are other issues with the leadership of corporations. They like to talk about the "30 000 foot view" implying that they have a great overview of the company and although they understand the details, it would take far too much time to explain them. I can tell you that the 30 000 foot view part is correct. That's the distance they choose to keep from the actual workings of the organizations they purport to lead. It's like a condor claiming to manage an ants nest far below. They can barely see it, let alone tell what's going on inside. That's not just my opinion, it's been proven.

In the acclaimed study "The Iceberg of Ignorance", consultant Sidney Yoshida concluded:

"Only 4% of an organization's front line problems are known by top management, 9% are known by middle management, 74% by supervisors and 100% by employees…".

Just **4%** of problems are known to top managers

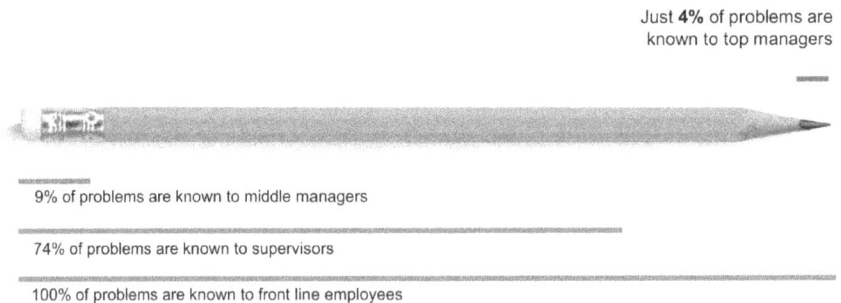

9% of problems are known to middle managers

74% of problems are known to supervisors

100% of problems are known to front line employees

Illustration of the astounding ignorance of top management

I realize that such people have a lot of demands on their time. However, if you are getting paid millions of dollars per year to lead, then perhaps it would be appropriate to understand the products you make, the developments in the pipeline and to actively seek valuable feedback from your employees. It is very rare indeed to see a leader do any of these activities, or one might even say duties. What do they do instead? They listen exclusively to the managers who report directly to them. That's very convenient because it keeps the number of required contacts down but what kind of information do they receive? They are receiving information exclusively from the politician types who are concerned with maintaining the status quo, and above all else, in protecting their own position. I sometimes wonder if the egos of CEOs are so fragile that they need to listen to a flock of sycophants. That would make an interesting study.

The press likes to talk about a few flamboyant leaders at companies that are presently successful. In contrast, the vast majority are very non-dynamic people who are there exactly because of that quality. I suspect the Pope is elected at an advanced age so they can be certain that any chance of significant change has been expunged. People at the top got there by being viewed as mature, reliable and steady. Surprises from them are unlikely. They get their information from the team of politicians vying for position below them. Those politicians usually got there, not by delivering results, but by maneuvering. Very wise leaders get their information from the actual shop floor workers because they are the ones who make the company run, create the new products and know where the problems are. As mentioned, such leaders are very rare. Bridgewater Associates is the only company I've ever heard of that truly embraces that ideal. It takes a great deal of bravery and dedication to stare reality in the face. Thus, the workers of most companies are either very frustrated or don't care because they have given up, or were too lazy to care in the first place.

The book The Innovator's DNA had something interesting to say on this topic. They said that top executives in large companies get there by delivering. Delivery skills are rewarded by late stage (mature) companies. In contrast, start-ups reward discovery skills. So large companies look for professional managers who follow procedures and implement processes. Younger companies need inventors and problem solvers who operate with great flexibility. That makes a lot of sense.

The book goes on to make some suggestions that seem nonsensical to me. They propose that the leaders should learn to become inventive through practice, which is in my view and according to studies, very unlikely to happen because creativity is genetic and can't be learnt. They even say that workers should try to maintain creativity during their career because it will be handy when they make it to the top. The problem is that companies act to instantly quash any sign of creativity. I have yet to work for a company where it was possible to deliver innovation and get promoted for it. Quite frankly, demonstrations of creativity will scare your managers and they will make sure they prevent any further challenges to the status quo. You will certainly not make it to the top of any larger corporation through displays of creativity.

For the last couple of decades, I have felt that the middle managers were holding back innovation. I heard CEOs implore us to deliver it and some of us tried to deliver but it was as though all progress was stifled by the middle management. I had no evidence to back up my impression that the middle managers were too conservative. Then, while writing this book, I read the excellent book Originals by Adam Grant. Adam has a brilliant writing style and he backs up his theories with evidence, so there is real substance to his revelatory works. Anyway, while reading Originals, I was amazed to discover they have studied the behavior of middle managers. It has been shown that they are indeed risk averse but not for the reason I had imagined. I had assumed that they picked conservative people for middle management positions in an attempt to preserve the status quo. In fact, those people change and become conservative once promoted. It was found that middle managers are so eager to protect their position that they don't dare to take any risks.

The Innovator's DNA: Mastering the Five Skills of Disruptive Innovators, Jeff Dyer, Hal Gregersen, Clayton M. Christensen, Harvard Business Review Press, USA 2011.

Originals: How Non-Conformists Move the World, Adam M. Grant, Viking (Random House), New York USA, 2016.

Size Matters

"The biggest obstacle to innovation is a paid off plant."

A presenter at the Ionic Liquids conference in 2006 made that comment and the audience broke out in spontaneous laughter. Laughter aside, the message is a serious one. A new manufacturing process or product has to beat the incumbent one, for which the investment has already been made. Not only that, but the incumbent has been optimized year after year, in some cases, for decades. A 20 or 30 year head start is a lot to overcome. Such an example came up at BASF. A revolutionary way to make one of their plastics was investigated and although all the calculations showed it was probably superior, the advantage was not overwhelming enough to overcome the resistance to change.

The huge scale of manufacturing and colossal size of companies these days introduces significant problems. The processes have evolved to run on world-scale plants costing hundreds of millions to build. They started off at pilot scale decades ago and grew step by step over time. Every new generation of factory got larger, in manageable steps and with every step, the manufacturing cost for the product became a little lower.

I'm a chemist by training, so let's consider a proposed new chemical process to make an established commodity product. There is no way for such a process to scale gradually in order to become competitive. In order to enjoy the economy of scale that the existing process has. It would have to make a gargantuan leap from pilot plant directly to a world-scale plant. Especially in the world of chemical processes, scaling is a risky business and such a leap would be career-endingly foolhardy. For other manufacturing methods that do scale predictably, the investment would still be too great and besides, what do you do with the old paid-off plant it is replacing? These practical but powerful obstacles to change are not usually discussed.

There are other serious drawbacks to large organizations. Did you know it has been shown that social groups break down when they become too large? It is referred to as Dunbar's Number. For humans it is approximately 150 people. Beyond that size, people are unable to keep up the large number of interactions needed to maintain strong enough relationships for the social group to work. The workplace is a social group and will cease to operate properly once it is too large.

Analogously, it has been shown that the design of each animal is tuned with respect to its size. A mouse as large as an elephant would not survive (see On Being the Right Size by J. B. S. Haldane). It's the same for single cell bacteria. They can only grow so large before the surface area is not great enough to bring in all the oxygen and nutrients required for the increasing volume of the cell as it expands.

Some organizations have recognized the importance of keeping units at a workable size. HP for example, would split a business unit once it had reached a certain size (revenue in that case). The Swedish tax authority announced that they would erect separate buildings with working space and parking facilities for 150 people each, i.e. Dunbar's Number.

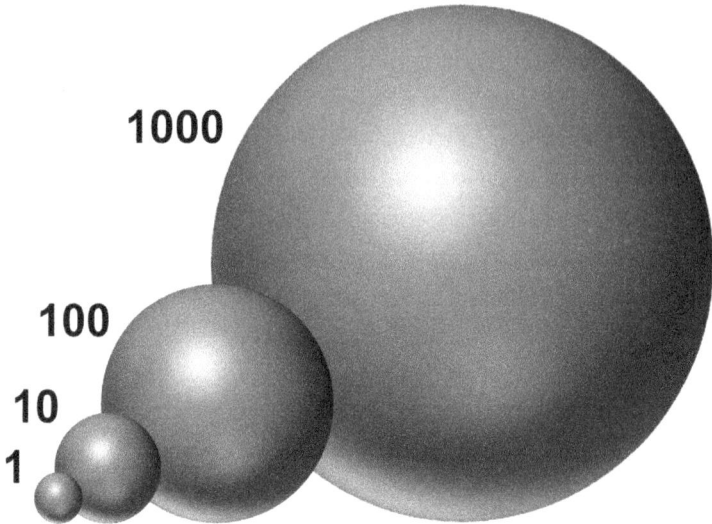

Companies of 1, 10, 100 and 1000 employees represented by the volume of a sphere

I like to visualize each company as a sphere. The surface area represents contact to the outside world. For a company, that means contact with customers. The volume of the sphere represents the number of employees and internal contacts to other employees. Employees on the surface have interactions both outside the organization and also back to those within the organizational sphere. Sales people would be typical surface dwelling employees in this model. The diagram helps us to visualize companies of 1, 10, 100 and 1000 employees.

The table shows how the numbers scale as we increase the number of employees. For Phantom Plastics, my small company of one, this model predicts that I spend a similar amount of time on external contacts and tasks as I do on internal company work. It estimates that for every one unit of time spent on internal tasks, I spend about 1.2 units doing customer related activities. For a company of 100 we see that about a quarter of the company contacts and work are externally focused. That is still a reasonable ratio and companies of 100 employees can do very well. However, for a very large company like BASF or Electrolux we see that less than 3% of the company is in direct contact with the outside world.

Number of Employees (sphere volume)	Exposure to Outside (sphere surface area)	Proportion of External Contact (surface area:volume)
1	1.2	120%
10	5.6	56%
100	26	26%
1,000	121	12%
10,000	560	5.6%
100,000	2600	2.6%

The numbers seem fairly realistic to me but the exact numbers are not the main point. It's the scaling concept that matters. We all know that in a large company you're stuck in internal meetings all day and wrapped up in red tape. It takes all your effort just to deal with the rules, the politics and so on. That's because, in a big company, almost all the work is internal. Not only does it slow you down but it also means no-one has any clue what the customer wants because only a very few employees actually spend any time with customers. This also explains why large companies are full of "politicians". When almost every contact is internal, those people who are good at playing corporate games do well. They bring nothing of benefit to the company though, which is what they are paid to do. In contrast, those employees that focus their energy on delivering results for the company don't get ahead because they are not spending enough time playing the corporate games. Thus, as we saw, the people with the potential to do the most good are also the ones most likely to get laid off.

When there is too little contact to the outside world, the company cannot survive. It is ironic that companies strive to grow and then, as they grow larger and falter, their strategy is to try to merge and become even larger. That is just the opposite of what they need. At the time of writing, Dow and DuPont are merging. That's an event worth considering. Two companies that got so big as to be ineffectual, for all the reasons we've discussed. So, what is their answer? Their great plan is to merge to become even larger and even more useless. Just for fun I just checked and yes, they both use Taleo®. A handy barometer of their attitude to employees and, in my view, an indication of their prospects for the future.

The Government is the biggest organization of all and therefore they are even more hopeless than the large corporations. A friend who worked in research for the US military told me some vivid stories of waste and ineptitude. The people in the R&D there are obliged to come up with problems to post so that companies and universities can apply for SBIR funding (an acronym for Small Business Innovation Research). The boss would come around and say, "quick, think of some project to post" and the workers would obligingly come up with something. Something that no-one really needed and to be funded with our tax-payers' money.

One worker there decided to use the official procedure to requisition a refrigerator. Of course no-one used the official procedure, because it was far too cumbersome. He decided it would be amusing to try it and see what happened. So, he filled in all the masses of paperwork to get his fridge. Then he waited…

Seven years later, a man arrived and declared that there was a refrigerator to be delivered, only to be told that the prankster had left the base four years prior. An impressive waste of time and money. Seven years of administration work paid for with our tax money. A happy thought indeed.

For similar reasons, government funded innovation makes no sense. This is how it operates. First the government takes away your profit in the form of taxes. Then they give you the opportunity to apply for your own money back again to do some research. You fill out tons of paperwork and someone who has very little understanding of the needs of industry screens the applications and decides who gets the money. Of course, only a fraction of the tax money is given back because there's a sizeable administration fee. My suggestion would be to leave the money with the companies, because they earned it and have a much better idea what they need to spend it on than some government administrator does. An official investigation some years ago concluded the same.

> "...the Hoover Task Force has found the government incompetent to perform even military research and development, much less civilian."
> Murray N. Rothbard in Science, Technology, & Government

Size does of course have its advantages but they are rather widely recognized. A large company may have more marketing clout and purchasing leverage for example. People may be attracted to them for their widespread reputation. There is also a certain perceived security in belonging to such a large group, although I would argue that is illusory. If anything, large companies tend to be less competitive and lay-offs are commonplace. When I lived in Sweden, first Ericsson, then Electrolux, had huge lay-offs flooding the market with qualified candidates. There were over 200 applicants for one job I applied for in Stockholm that year.

There is another unmentioned problem with large companies. It is close to impossible to really make a difference there. By that I mean a game-changing difference that impacts the bottom line. Look at a company with 5 billion per year in revenue, even a monumentally successful new product will hardly move the needle. Given that it's extremely hard to push through a change in a large company, as we have shown, and given that it won't make a difference anyway. What's the point in trying?

Having worked in companies from 80,000 employees all the way down to under 50, or my own one man consulting company, Phantom Plastics, I've experienced it all. So, I will describe what I've seen. The small companies are nimble. It's obvious but it does make a huge practical difference. The small company cares because what each person does makes a difference. Also, smaller companies attract people who believe in their own ability to make that difference. I have many examples, but here is one. One of my favorite plastics additives is called ultrahigh molecular weight silicone. A mouthful I know, so it's known as UHMW silicone. It's a great product and it has been marketed by two major corporations for well over a decade (Dow Corning and Wacker). I recommended it to a client and contacted both companies to request a sample. It was urgent and neither of them got back to me right away. By chance, a small company contacted me, unsolicited, and said they sold it. It was an amazing coincidence. I ordered a sample and it was on my doorstep at 9am the next morning. I was impressed. So what of the other two requests? Dow Corning never responded and Wacker's distributor eventually called me two weeks later. Too late. The small company was proactive, fast, friendly and cheaper! They cared because every sale means income for themselves and their families. In contrast, employees of big companies do not really care.

A friend at a very large and famous corporation had something to add on this topic. He said it was not just the size of the company that counted but also the level of desperation. He has been in that same large company for decades and been through a few economic up and down cycles. What he observed is that in good times there is no sense of urgency and no real focus on R&D. In effect, they rest of their laurels in good times. Then, when profits plummet, suddenly the sense of urgency is back and there is renewed emphasis on getting out new breakthrough products. It may be that smaller companies are not good at innovating only because they are small but also because they tend to be more desperate. Start-ups for example don't know whether they will make their next funding round. It was an interesting perspective. I wanted to share it and I thank him for alerting me to that piece of wisdom.

So, what size does a company have to be before things start to break down? Let us consider one company I followed over a couple of decades. First they had years of success by being smaller, nimble and hungry. Then they slowly turned into a normal company of a few hundred employees, driven by rules, full of politics, bullying, dishonesty and ineffectiveness. You may think I'm exaggerating so let me elucidate. One person explained how they would bribe customers without it being caught on their expense report. It was reported to three separate people in senior management, but no-one cared. This is the kind of complacency and lack of ethics that brings down companies as they grow. Their marketing literature was full of mistakes. The mistakes were reported and two years later they were still there. A whole marketing team drawing salary and yet unable to do professional work or make simple corrections. Another time HR reported that a worker had lied on their resume. They had claimed to have a degree when in fact they had barely attended college at all. Again, management didn't care. Of course they had all of the usual "we're so ethical" stuff in their employee handbook but that was just for show it seems.

Perhaps the most impressively dynamic company I have ever seen is Tactus Technology. They have created and patented a mobile device touch screen that has invisible buttons that pop up on demand to give you a tactile experience, i.e. you can actually push the buttons and get that positive feedback people want. Then, the buttons vanish when no longer needed. I have consulted for them for a number of years and they amaze me with their speed, drive and how smart a bunch of people they have. It's electrifying to meet them and to sense the spirit and talent in their small office in California. Being that good doesn't guarantee success but it sure does help.

Another small impressive company I have worked with is Virtuix who make a revolutionary virtual reality apparatus that you can walk around in while remaining stationary so you don't collide with your walls and other objects in the real world. Their drive, focus and speed to market was inspirational. They cared. Of the larger companies, there are only a couple that stand out as being responsive. Apple is one. They are fast and their demands on their suppliers are such that suppliers create elite teams just to deal with the rapid pace that Apple demands.

THE DANGER OF SAFETY

"He who doesn't take risks, doesn't drink champagne."

An old Russian proverb

It seems very natural to assume that safety must be a good thing. For example, when the industrial revolution came, there were children working in factories and far too many accidents. However, over the decades, that has changed dramatically to the point where we have far, far, too much emphasis on safety. That may sound impossible, but let me explain. I will present plenty of examples, to make sure the point is convincingly made.

We all know that pretty much everything in life is a question of balance. We know that oxygen is good and we need it to live. However, if you breathe pure oxygen, you feel great for a while and then you die. Too much of a "good" thing. The same has happened with the topic of safety in companies, partly because no-one can stand up and argue against safety. It sounds callous and strange. So, year after year, the safety imperative has grown to the point that it is almost impossible to work. I'm not kidding. If you ask anyone working in R&D about safety, they will instantly be able to give you "amusing" examples of how the system has broken down. I know because I have asked and I will relate some of those examples now to show you just how bad it is. Insiders get a laugh out of sharing these stories but at the same time, we know it's not really funny at all because it stops us and our companies from being effective. Innovation is stopped in its tracks.

Before I relate stories from several Fortune 500 companies and from my own experience, I would like to point out examples that everyone can relate to from everyday life. Every time I am on an airplane they have a, frankly absurd, safety announcement. They warm up by telling us not to congregate in the aisles and about the life vests we will never need. Then it gets worse. We are told not to "tamper with, disable or destroy the smoke detectors". I have news for them, you can't disable or destroy something without tampering with it. You're telling me the same thing three times. Finally, that's over and the pretzels and nuts come around and I laugh again because the peanuts have an interesting warning on the back. It says "this product was produced in a facility that processes peanuts and other nuts". Amazing! All this time I thought peanuts were processed in a bicycle factory! Not to mention that a peanut is not a nut, it's a legume and grows underground, so the rest of the sentence is wrong too. The dry roasted peanuts are from the King Nut Company and come in a shiny red package. You can see them too if you fly Delta. Apparently they feel their customers are morons, or perhaps their lawyers are.

As I have been taking notes for this book over the last several years, I have made a point of collected stories from people I know at major corporations. If you are a senior manager, you may be smugly thinking that none of this applies to your company. Think again. This picture is universal across the Fortune 500 and other large companies. Don't believe me? Give me the telephone number of someone in your R&D and I will call them and get the stories of how safety is killing your company. So, here we go...

A researcher at a household name company was in the habit of cycling to work. One day he had a puncture and took his bike back to the lab to repair it. He had the inner tube out and had located the puncture. It's a scene we're all familiar with. Just as he was applying that vital one drop of rubber cement, the safety inspection people happened to walk in. He was written up and fined for "working with a solvent not in a fume cupboard" (a fume cupboard is like a ventilated desk that sucks away smells). Amazing. Children use that glue at home but in a lab setting that somehow becomes a finable safety violation.

A large plastics company bought a new piece of mixing equipment called an extruder. It was too heavy for their electrically operated forklifts, so they needed to use a propane powered forklift, which is actually the more common type. As their safety people were unfamiliar with those forklifts, they decided they must surely be deadly and give off toxic gasses. In actuality, burning propane is very safe, which is why we use it to cook food on our gas grills. After weeks of meetings, delays and planning it was decided they could use the propane forklift but only if the whole facility was evacuated and all the doors and windows were opened to prevent poisoning the employees with the (imaginary) toxic gasses. Another example of needlessly wasted money and time.

When I was at BASF I witnessed similar events. One time they bought a glove box which is standard equipment used in labs and hospitals everywhere. Glove boxes allow you to handle oxygen sensitive substances. The safety people decided this equipment, which is well regarded and good enough for everyone else, was not good enough for them. They spent months taking it apart to replace wires, motors and other parts on the brand new equipment. No-one could understand it, the scientists had no choice but to watch in wonder at the expense and delay to their project.

On a trip to a large oil company I saw more bizarre systems. I was with an employee and we pulled up to the gate where a security officer asked for his employee badge, registered us, gave us an ID card each and then raised the gate so the car could enter. That seemed reasonable enough. What happened next is what caught me by surprise. We drove around 100 yards to a parking spot and walked a few steps to the front entrance of the building. There we saw the usual reception desk. The lady asked us for our badges, the ones that we had received 60 seconds earlier and took our details in order to issue us each with another ID badge. Doesn't anyone in management think this is a shocking waste of time and resources? Are they all asleep at the helm? Is no-one checking to see whether the procedures are sensible? Apparently not. Once inside it was more of the same. Signs that said "Stop! Are you more than 6 feet off the ground? Tether yourself or get down immediately". This was in an ordinary office environment, not a mountaineering expedition. Then of course they had the obligatory "always use the handrail when using the stairs" signs. Again, companies seem to believe they have hired a busload of school children. After the meeting, we wanted lunch and I asked whether we could go to the restaurant. My host explained that would be tricky because once in there we would have no way to get back into the main building without exiting and walking a long distance around the perimeter to re-enter at reception. Who dreams up this stuff?

At many companies you have to watch a 5 to 10 minute safety video and pass a test before entering the facility. One of my friends said it's quite absurd because, even as an employee of the company, it's a challenge to remember the stuff they try to teach a visitor in just a few minutes. His example was "if you hear a horn with 6 long blasts then it means there has been a chemical leak and you need to evacuate, but if you hear 5 long blasts followed by three shorter blasts then it's some other kind of emergency". Really? Why would the visitor be walking around unattended anyway? All visitors should be with their host and would just need to follow them if something happens. Simple. Too simple apparently.

I thought this safety trend was a new development so I made a point of asking an older semi-retired friend who worked at the famous UK chemical company ICI. He related how it was in the 1990s. Perhaps you remember Bunsen burners from your school days? Well, at ICI you had to fill out a hazardous equipment form and take that to the chemical store room in order to borrow a Bunsen burner. So, even back in the 90s, graduates and PhD chemists had to jump through hoops to borrow equipment that any 16-year-old can use at school.

In many companies they have a rule that every meeting has to begin with a comment on safety. So, the presenter will stand up and say "it's icy on the roads today, drive safely". Again, the companies must be convinced that they have morons working for them. However, the workers are (usually) not morons, they don't appreciate being treated like morons and they immediately lose respect for the company enforcing such mindless mantras.

When I was selling minerals at another company I was, on two separate occasions, asked whether the mineral was explosive. I wonder what these people see when they look out of their kitchen window into their garden. Apparently, the rocks, i.e. minerals, in their garden are exploding on a regular basis. I told them minerals are not explosive but they wanted to see the data. I explained that an explosion is a very rapid combustion and that the particular mineral under discussion is sold for its flame retardant properties. Not only is it not combustible but it actually helps extinguish fires. Did that satisfy them? Nope. I had to get the safety person at our company to issue a statement, on our letterhead, that it was not explosive.

Another example is from a producer of high performance plastics. I had a really fruitful presentation and meeting with about ten of their experts, several of whom requested samples. I walked away encouraged and ready to send the samples. The next day I was surprised to get an email declaring that the mineral I had shown them was unsafe and not TSCA listed, so they could not touch it. Everyone who had been at the meeting was copied. Of course, if this person had actually been competent, he would have known how ridiculous his statement was. I took the time to point out that the company I represented sold several billion dollars of that mineral every year to companies all around the world so we would be aware of any such safety issue. I also pointed out that all natural minerals are TSCA listed by definition and sent him the regulations with that section highlighted. It amazed me that I had to send the safety regulations to them. How can they claim to be enforcing regulations when apparently, they have not read them?

I assume he was convinced on that point because he moved on to present other objections. First he asked whether the mineral was corrosive, again copying everyone. I explained that it was not an issue. Then he wrote back saying that surely there was no way this mineral could be used in plastics. I said in that case we had better call BMW and tell them to stop making cars because they had been using it for years.

The whole experience was a waste of everyone's time and all because the safety person apparently felt driven to try and prevent any attempt at making progress. A lot of the momentum built up in my initial meeting was lost in the exchange. We never did make any progress. Soon after, McKinsey & Company were sent in and large layoffs ensued. I checked and the inept safety obsessed person survived the cuts while some of the R&D people he thwarted were let go.

I have a lot more of these stories but let's stop here and reflect. We have seen that safety people are slowing or completely preventing progress. Often they don't even know the rules but somehow feel they are the gatekeepers of progress. As a consequence, progress is slowed and momentum is lost. In the worst case, R&D is slowed down so much that cuts are made and all hope of innovation is then gone. There are other, less obvious consequences. One is that the creative people, that deliver breakthrough ideas, are allergic to red tape. I know because I am one of those people. They don't want to work in a company where progress is very slow, or impossible, so they leave.

A company I worked at had a mission statement prominently featuring the words "Safety First". If your company really puts safety before everything else, then I don't want to be a shareholder. It should be "make money first and be safe while you're at it." The year on year goal of a lower accident rate produces very bad, unintended results. More on that below.

Let's go back to my experiences at BASF's HQ in Ludwigshafen Germany. They have a giant factory there with over 30 000 people including R&D and other functions. They were very keen on safety. In R&D we had a monthly meeting where we would discuss every accident that had occurred on the site. It was tedious and unproductive. In short, a waste of time.

More worrying though was what happened when there was an accident. One worker had an accident that prevented him from driving to work. What did they do? They paid for a taxi for 30 miles to work and 30 miles to take him home, not just for one day but for weeks. Of course he couldn't work due to his injury, so why did they go to all that expense? Simple, the bonuses of the top management depend on the number and severity of accidents reported. They will do anything to make sure the record shows no accidents.

I saw the same behavior up close when one of my own workers cut his hand with a spatula. He decided to stay at home to recuperate and the managers went into a panic. As his boss, I had to fill out an accident form and I started to see where the panic came from. The form had three boxes for different accidents of different severities. Box number one was for accidents necessitating one day or less off work. The second box was for 2-3 days off work. The last box was for people who took more than three days off work or were dead. So, taking more than three days off with a cut thumb was counted the same in the accident stats as being dead. My boss called my worker at home and made it very clear that it would be to everyone's benefit if he came to work. He got the message and showed up to work the next day. Of course he couldn't work, but the big boss's bonus was saved. Thank goodness.

Every company I have worked at had such a vanishingly low accident rate that it was almost impossible to improve upon it. Yet, the mandate was to lower the accident rate every single year. As that's the target and that's what up to 30% of the top managements bonus is based on, you can bet they will do anything to make the numbers look good, even if it means cheating. I wanted to see whether this was an isolated practice, or something more widespread. I asked around at a few major companies and discovered that they do exactly the same. When someone is injured, they get them a taxi to work and have them sit in a room playing computer games so that they don't miss work and thereby ruin the site's accident record. One particular site had an outstanding record for just that reason, until one day, a fatality ruined it. Apparently, they haven't yet found a way to hide that kind of accident.

A friend pointed out to me that if people are afraid to report accidents, then accident prevention suffers. Ideally, all accidents and near misses would be reported, so that appropriate actions are taken to improve safety. When the accident records are being falsified, then this prevention mechanism is stymied. Ironically, the attempt to appear safe, actually lowers a company's ability to be safe.

One of my good friends said that his safety representative asked him whether he thought it was possible to have an accident rate of zero. My friend honestly and correctly stated "no, that is not possible". To which the safety person replied "that's the problem, people don't believe it's possible and that's what's holding us back". They then embarked on a campaign to try and convince the workers that an accident rate of zero is realistic. Are these people mentally deficient or just incredibly naive? Increasing safety costs money and slows down work. It can be viewed as a tax on your productivity. It should be clear to anyone of modest intelligence that safety is good up to a point and that a balance is needed. A 100% safe company would have a productivity of zero and would go out of business.

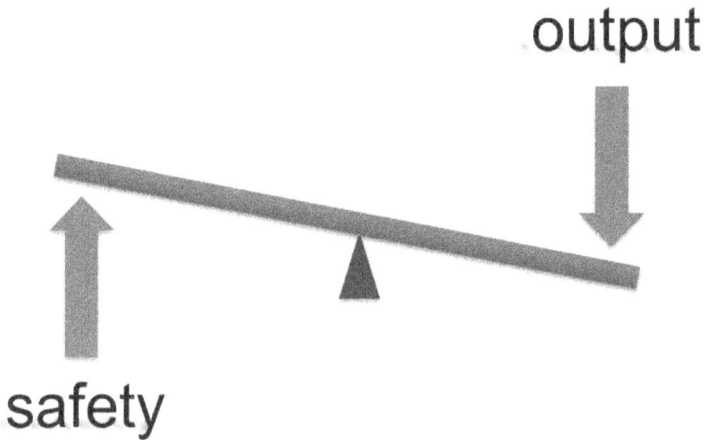

The effect of safety is to decrease output, so a balance is needed

At another company, the top managers have to do a set number of safety tours per year at the factories. However, some of the managers are stationed at offices, not factories making it hard for them to reach their target. So, when there is a company meeting at a factory, all the managers stroll around in a gaggle so they can meet their target and get their bonus. Not a great use of time for presidents and business unit heads. If the company sets silly targets, then people will do anything to meet them. It is therefore critical to set meaningful targets instead.

The only way to be truly safe is to stay at home wrapped in cotton. The idea of perfect safety at work has turned into a cancer spreading without control and slowly killing the host. Have a look at the amount your company has spent on so-called safety and how it has mushroomed over the last few decades. Companies should save money by cutting back on the safety personnel. Then, they need to make sure that those remaining are working to help innovation and that they actually know the rules they are supposed to enforce.

Earlier we mentioned the invention of the special polyethylene called Dyneema® that is five times stronger than steel. Here's what one of the team had to say in the article Romancing the Thread: the Story of Dyneema®.

"With today's rules for safety and control, it would be almost impossible to bring something like Dyneema® to the market."
Jos Schneiders

I would suggest that safety overhead should be no more than 1% of the revenue. After all, R&D is often just 1-3%. Safety should be fast but effective and never slow down projects. It is best applied to factories and not to creative activities. Bachelor degree and PhD scientists in your R&D are already trained in safety during their studies. Company boards need to make sure they don't set bonuses based on safety because it encourages undesirable behavior. If you work in safety, remember you are there to help the company progress, not to slow everything down. If you are an innovator in a company ruled by an overbearing safety mantra, my advice is to leave that company.

I removed some of the examples I had written to keep the length down but I will post them at www.innovationabyss.com and invite you to post your own there. Maybe if we expose the severity of this problem, companies may wake up and do something.

CONCLUSIONS

Conclusions

On this journey together, we have seen that every part of the innovation process is broken, which is why the success rate for launching innovative new products is extraordinarily low. Your company and all your competitors stumble along year after year with no sign of improvement. You know that you need innovation to get an edge and then to stay ahead, but it remains elusive. The reason being that, despite all the articles and books, no-one, until now, has pinpointed the real problems that strangle innovation. Thus, the Innovation Abyss sucks in endless money, creativity, effort and time. Ironically, it reminds me of the infamous innovation funnel diagram, except that nothing ever emerges from the Innovation Abyss.

As you realize by now, this is not a feel good book. I'm not here to amuse anyone or repeat the usual platitudes. Instead, I have shared the horrifying stories of an insider who has seen the innovation battles fought and usually lost, over the last thirty years.

I set out to write this book with a set of firm beliefs, based on my own experience. I was convinced that I could point out where the true problems are but I wanted more than that, so I went looking for proof. I was shocked to learn that many of the topics have been studied. It's proven that Stage Gate doesn't work. Six Sigma doesn't either. It's been proven that middle managers really do hold back progress. Most importantly it has been proven that there are certain individuals that can give you a ten fold higher return on your R&D dollars. Those people are easy to identify when you know how. Perhaps the most tragic part is that all the information is there and virtually no-one is using it. This book aims to correct that. Having read it, you now have proven tools to get dramatically better results, leading to a profitable future and a sustainable edge.

"There are three categories of people in industry – the few who make things happen, the many who watch things happen, and the overwhelming majority who have no idea what happened."

Orlando A. Battista

Which do you want to be?

ACTIONS AND ADVICE

A dvice to innovators: by all means start in a large company to get exposed to the environment and learn. You can benchmark yourself against your colleagues and see whether you thrive in that environment or not. Then, if you want to make a difference and are brave, get out to a small or medium sized company that will give you the freedom to deliver and will probably reward you for it.

Advice to middle managers: your job is to help the people under you be the best they can be, to remove road blocks and give recognition and promotion to those that try hard to make progress. If you don't have "NT" in your Meyers-Briggs personality profile, then you probably shouldn't be managing innovation. You will be uncomfortable and ineffectual. Don't be afraid to take risks, you were promoted because someone thought you displayed good judgement. Keep taking calculated risks that add value.

Advice to senior managers / leaders: only with you as a champion can innovation succeed. You are the only ones with influence over the entire organization to encourage the right environment and to make sure the units work together to pass the innovation "baton" along and run a successful race. You are paid big money to be brave and make a difference, so do it. Stop reorganizing and you will gain significant efficiency over your competitors who remain in a needless state of flux. Spend more time listening to your regular employees than to the managers directly below you.

Advise to board members: people will play the game by the rules you set and the senior management tend to be smart people. Instead of allowing them to get their bonuses based on criteria of safety or quality (and tempt them to fake it), base it on something that is substantial and helps the company like revenue from products created within the last 3 years. Monitor to ensure the metrics are reported correctly. Give a small base salary and lots of options, like the Disney example where sustainable success is rewarded over short-term thinking.

Advice to companies: do basic benchmarking to test that your company is healthy. Have someone external try to set up an NDA. If it takes more than 2 weeks to sign your own NDA, there is a problem. Have someone submit a web inquiry. If it takes more than 1-2 days to get answered (let alone months), that's unacceptable. Have someone apply for a job and track their progress. Do they get a reply? Does their résumé land on someone's desk? If not, that's a major problem. Ask for examples of people who were fired for being dishonest. If your company really is ethical then there will be examples. If no-one has been fired, then that's a danger sign. Do 360 degree evaluations for all staff so you can find out which managers are causing problems. Pay your difference makers top dollar to stay with you. They are very rare and give you an enormous edge. Don't make them leave to go help your competition.

Appendix: Being an Innovator in a Large Corporation

I showed a draft of this book to a close friend and he said he would like to see a section on being an innovator in a large corporation. It's very handy to have someone to point out what you have missed. So, here are some thoughts on what I have experienced and what advice I might give to a younger me.

First, how do you know that you might be an innovator at heart? Here's something I read recently which describes my view of the world.

"Start with the assumption that the best way to do something is not the way it's being done right now."

Aaron Levie, Box

If that describes you, then read on because you may well be an innovator. You might also try the creativity tests mentioned earlier. The good news is that you don't need to have the highest IQ to be creative. A certain level of intelligence is needed but it reaches a plateau after that.

During my time in Stockholm I attended a lecture by Dr. Dusan Prevorsek, a well-known scientist. He said that he was part of a study to find out why some academic high fliers become successful and others vanish into obscurity. The study showed that three factors were vital. Your first boss, your first project and your first job. The ideal strategy they found was to join a large corporation in order to gain experience but to stay there no longer than two years. Then go out and make your mark in a smaller company. The advice rings true in my view. Firstly, one needs to understand the real world problems and how organizations operate. Also, it is essential to build a network. Therefore, the idea of starting off in a large company has merit. However, your chance of making an impact in a large organization is almost zero. Plus, as we have seen, even if you were to do so, you would not get compensated for it. Therefore, it is essential to join a smaller company, where your contribution is much more likely to be valued. In later years, forming your own company may be a wise option. If you are an ideas person, try to team up with people who can help bring your ideas to fruition (see the book Rocket Fuel by Wickman and Winters for more on that).

What other advice would I give to a young innovator? Try very hard to get a good manager who supports you. They are rare. About one out of three of my managers has been "good" and the rest were either lackluster or egocentric office politicians. Try to get a project that truly interests you and is a priority to the company. Build up your network as much as you can. Also, it is essential to have a thorough understanding of your subject area, as that is the foundation upon which you then build. If that is shaky, then you will run into problems. After the foundation of understanding is built, then focus on collecting information. Nowadays, information is so abundant that what you are actually looking for is outliers. Normal information is just a Google search away, so there is no need to memorize that. Instead, take particular note of the unusual and value that over the normal. In that way you can collect and store useful nuggets for later use. The same applies to your experiments. When an experiment goes as expected, little is learnt but when the unexpected occurs, pay close attention. Do not fall into the trap of thinking of it as a failed experiment. Ask yourself why it went as it did and whether you can commercialize this accidental discovery. Some of my best discoveries were failed attempts to do something else. Other high value materials I have developed came from reading books. Scientists discover and report amazing new materials but fail to recognize the commercial potential. If you have the skills, you can bring them to market.

In researching for this book, I read and listened to the opinions of some thought leaders and was surprised by what two of them said. These are very rich entrepreneurs who built their own businesses. They agreed that you should work to your strengths. Robert Herjavec said that, at school, they teach us to correct our weaknesses. The teacher may say "your handwriting isn't good enough, you need to practice that". So, we are taught to work on what we're intrinsically least good at. In essence that means we are working towards becoming average at everything! My handwriting is indeed poor, so should I spend hundreds of hours working on it? Why strive toward mediocrity when the difference makers are the few outliers? The advice of those experts was to take what you already excel at and work on that to become world-class because that is when you can make an impact and be successful. I agree.

> *"Find your one thing and do that one thing better than anyone else."*
> Jason Goldberg, Fab.com

I am often asked how I go about solving problems and I invariably answer that I go looking for them. You need to find a genuine problem in order to get started. Innovating in a vacuum is very hard to do. So-called "pure" scientists may enjoy solving problems that no-one cares about but that does not suit me at all. I like to see the happy customer when I have helped them, knowing that it really means something to them and their company. That is a large part of what drives me, plus I like the buzz of proving to myself that I can do it.

This is something you can read elsewhere but the key is to find what you love. If you are passionate, you will be the best. No-one who is just doing it for a job, i.e. to pay the bills, will be better than you. Books will tell you to learn continuously but that's nonsense. It's nonsense to tell you that because if you are passionate, you will automatically devote lots of energy in your quest to learn and be the best. If you are not working with something you love, no book can make you become passionate. It doesn't work that way. It's the same with the books and courses that tell you to be creative. Utter rubbish. You're either an idea machine, or you're not.

I once read about a study that said that there is a way to tell who is a true expert. The real expert will tell you when they don't know the answer. The delusional, fake expert, will claim to know everything. I found that interesting and I have also found it to be true. The real expert has the self-confidence and honesty to say when they don't know. The pretenders will make false statements leading to problems such as a confused client. Know your stuff and be honest. When you don't know, say so.

I have also found that a true expert is able to explain complex topics in simple terms. The pretender is prone to hide their ignorance and insecurity behind long words and techno-babble. I was taught polymer science by Professor Norman Billingham and he was a master at making any topic both simple and enjoyable. He showed me the way. I now do quite a bit of training for companies including the Fortune 100. Customers often compliment me on making it so simple to understand. They assume I am dumbing it down for them but the way I describe it is actually the same way I visualize polymers, materials, chemicals and so on. When you truly understand something, it becomes rather simple. I hope that you too can help simplify the complex and train the next generation to be fascinated by science so they can help create a better future.

Another trait of the passionate expert is the desire to be around and learn from the best. Where others may feel threatened by the legends in their field, for me it is thrilling to be around the best. After all, they are the people who are by far the most likely to teach me something new. They are also the most likely to challenge my views and convince me to change my mind. My closest friends include Professor Roger Rothon (he is the reason that this chapter exists), Dr. Graham McKee (retired from BASF with 210 patents) and others who I value for their intelligence, creativity, passion and strong ethics.

Work where it's safe to take risks. Companies are asking you to innovate, which means change and people are frightened of change. So try to work in places and companies who will support you while you are innovating. This reminds me of an article entitled "Don't Fire Me: I'm Innovating" which cited a study showing that US states that protect the employees have higher quality patents. In many US states, hiring is "at will" meaning you can be fired at any time with no reason needed. I would recommend that innovators consider working in one of the European countries like Sweden, Italy or Germany where job security is much higher.

"If everything seems under control, you're just not going fast enough."

Mario Andretti

As well as decreasing the risk to innovators, we must increase their reward. As we have seen, in a normal corporate position, you are unlikely to receive any reward whatever for providing them with a money making breakthrough. The patent system was designed to reward the inventor personally but as we know, that has been hijacked by the employers who force us to sign away all of our rights in exchange for a paycheck. Nevertheless, there are some ways to get compensation for your ideas. Smaller companies may be willing to give you stock options. Sometimes it's possible to create your own side company, for example to do consulting. That approach has worked for me. It works well when your creativity extends beyond the areas that your employer is interested in. Then it's possible to clearly define what ideas belong to them and what areas are outside your employment and therefore yours to pursue. Employers are more likely to acquiesce if you have already got your own consulting company going when you apply for a job with them.

If you are really good at what you do, you may be bullied at some point in your career. Unlike playground bullying where the weaker children are bullied, in a business setting, it is the most competent that get bullied by bosses who are threatened by the superior skills of their subordinate. It has happened to me and I even wrote a LinkedIn post about bullying. To my surprise, several highly competent people wrote to me sharing their own rather scary stories. In my case I went to HR but received no help. Later I read that there is a 2% chance that HR will help you, with 37% of employees experiencing retaliation instead and 70% losing their job. Clearly, I made a mistake by telling HR. If it happens to you, find a new job before they get a chance to fire you.

Rocking the boat. That is what an innovator is being asked to do. What happens in a real boat when someone starts making it rock? People will be frightened and will probably ask them to stop. If they don't stop, then I would imagine their shipmates would throw them overboard. The same applies in companies. Be careful, or at least aware, of that risk.

I should also say some words about ego, arrogance and confidence. Having run larger projects with all types of personalities and people from different countries, I got a chance to witness their contributions to the project. Here's what I saw. Some people and indeed nationalities, tend to be more extroverted. I have seen meetings derailed by extroverts confidently stating views far beyond their competence level. In essence, their belief in themselves was unjustly inflated. That could be termed over-confidence or even arrogance. Conversely, I would sometimes see a very clever person sit quietly in a meeting while the more extrovert people talked. Yet I could see a glimmer in their eye that made me suspect that the quiet person had something worthwhile to contribute. Perhaps they had the answer to our debate. That valuable contribution remained unmade. In both cases we see waste. Wasted effort following people who don't have the answer and the waste of the solution never heard. It seems to me that everyone should strive to strike a balance between their confidence and their competence in order that we get the best out of each person.

> *"When your confidence exceeds your competence,*
> *disaster is the consequence."*
>
> Chris DeArmitt

There is more to say on the topic of confidence. I think part of the reason that managers can feel threatened by top experts is that the expert is confident and that intimidates them.

Sometimes, as mentioned, a confident person can be labelled arrogant. To me arrogance is when you have an over-inflated view of yourself. That seems to be backed up by the dictionary definition. As we have just mentioned above, it is the duty of an expert to express an appropriate degree of confidence in their area of excellence. That is not arrogance because there is alignment between the confidence and the competence. If you are really good, do not proceed with false modesty because you will not be making your maximum contribution. Proceed instead with measured confidence and do your utmost to make a difference. Only a few dare.

FURTHER READING

Here are some old favorites of mine and some books I stumbled upon while researching for this book.

The Art of Non-Conformity – Chris Guillebeau

Originals – Adam Grant

Tribal Leadership – Dave Logan, John King & Halee Fischer-Wright

Orbiting the Giant Hairball – Gordon MacKenzie

Parkinson's Law – C. Northcote Parkinson

Galactic Effectuator – Jack Vance

ABOUT THE AUTHOR

Chris is passionate about innovating with plastics, minerals, specialty chemicals and materials in general. He creates new materials, brings them to market, solves problems and provides training to companies large and small.

If you ask him about hobbies, like all ENTJ type people, he will reply that his work is his hobby. Even so, he will confess a fondness for sci-fi and fantasy books from old masters like Jack Vance, James Branch Cabell and Ernest Bramah. He is a self-proclaimed hi-fi nut who appreciates "good" music of many kinds. He lives in a calm village near Cincinnati Ohio with his wife and family.

www.ingramcontent.com/pod-product-compliance
Lightning Source LLC
Chambersburg PA
CBHW031406180326
41458CB00043B/6627/J